CHAPTER 1:

To effectively harness the power of Python, it is essential to familiarize ourselves with the installation process and the establishment of a suitable development environment. Python's accessibility is further enhanced by its cross-platform compatibility, making it possible to run the language on a variety of operating systems, including Windows, macOS, and Linux. Each operating system has its own nuances when it comes to installation, but the underlying principles remain consistent.

For Windows users, the process begins with downloading the Python installer from the official Python website. The installer provides a user-friendly interface that guides users through the installation steps. It is crucial to select the option to add Python to the system PATH during installation. This step ensures that Python can be invoked from any command prompt window, streamlining the execution of Python scripts. Once the installation is complete, users can verify the installation by opening a command prompt and typing `python --version`. This command should return the version of Python that has been installed, confirming that the installation was successful.

macOS users can install Python using either the official installer available on the Python website or through the Homebrew package manager. The official installer provides a straightforward installation process with a graphical interface. After downloading the installer, users can follow the on-screen instructions to complete the installation. Alternatively, Homebrew users can execute the command `brew install python`, which automatically handles the installation process and configuration. Regardless of the method chosen, verifying the installation involves opening the Terminal application and executing `python3 --version`, as macOS typically differentiates between Python 2 and Python 3.

For Linux users, the installation process varies slightly depending on the distribution. Most Linux distributions come with Python pre-installed, but it is often necessary to install or upgrade to a specific version. Users can typically use their distribution's package manager to install Python. For instance, on Ubuntu-based distributions, the command `sudo apt-get install python3` will install Python 3. On Fedora, the command `sudo dnf install python3` serves a similar purpose. After installation, users can verify the Python version by executing `python3 --version` in the terminal.

Once Python is installed, setting up a development environment is the next critical step. A development environment consists of the tools and settings that facilitate efficient coding and debugging. An integrated development environment (IDE) or a code editor can significantly enhance the programming experience. Popular choices for Python development include PyCharm, Visual Studio Code, and Jupyter Notebook.

PyCharm, developed by JetBrains, is a powerful IDE tailored specifically for Python. It offers advanced features such as code completion, debugging, and integrated testing. The Community Edition of PyCharm is free and provides ample functionality for most Python development needs. Users can download PyCharm from the JetBrains website and follow the installation instructions to set up the IDE.

Visual Studio Code (VS Code) is a lightweight and highly customizable code editor developed by Microsoft. It supports a wide range of programming languages, including Python, and offers extensions that enhance its functionality. To use

VS Code for Python development, users need to install the Python extension from the VS Code marketplace. This extension provides features such as syntax highlighting, code linting, and debugging support.

Jupyter Notebook is a unique tool designed for interactive computing and data analysis. It allows users to create and share documents that contain live code, equations, visualizations, and narrative text. Jupyter Notebooks are particularly popular in data science and academic research due to their ability to combine code execution with explanatory text. To install Jupyter Notebook, users can use the Python package manager, pip, by running the command `pip install notebook`. Once installed, Jupyter can be launched from the command line by typing `jupyter notebook`, which opens a web-based interface for creating and managing notebooks.

With the development environment established, the next step is to write and execute our first Python script. A script is essentially a file containing Python code that can be executed by the interpreter. To begin, open your chosen code editor or IDE and create a new file with the `.py` extension, which denotes a Python script. For simplicity, let's write a basic script that prints "Hello, World!" to the screen.

In your new Python file, enter the following code:

```python
print("Hello, World!")
```

This script utilizes the `print()` function, which is a built-in Python function used to output text to the console. The string "Hello, World!" is enclosed in quotation marks, indicating that it is a string literal. When executed, the `print()` function sends this string to the standard output, which, in this case, is the console or terminal window.

To run the script, navigate to the directory containing the Python file using the command line or terminal. Execute the script by typing `python script_name.py`, where `script_name.py` is the name of your Python file. Upon execution, the console should display "Hello, World!" confirming that the script ran successfully. If you are using Python 3, ensure that you use `python3` instead of `python` in the command.

This initial foray into Python programming demonstrates the language's ease of use and sets the stage for more complex and engaging projects. With Python successfully installed and a basic script executed, you are now well-positioned to explore the language's broader capabilities and delve into more advanced topics.

Selecting an integrated development environment (IDE) or a code editor is a pivotal step in optimizing your Python programming experience. While there are numerous options available, the choice largely depends on personal preference and specific needs. IDEs such as PyCharm and Visual Studio Code are highly regarded for their extensive features, including debugging tools, syntax highlighting, and project management capabilities. PyCharm, developed by JetBrains, offers a comprehensive environment tailored specifically for Python development. It provides advanced features like code refactoring, integrated testing, and virtual environment support. Its professional edition includes additional functionalities for web development and data science. Visual Studio Code, on the other hand, is a versatile and lightweight editor developed by Microsoft. It supports a wide range of programming languages through extensions and is favored for its customizable interface and robust debugging tools.

For those who prefer a more minimalist approach, editors like Sublime Text and Atom offer a streamlined coding experience. Sublime Text is known for its speed and efficiency, featuring a distraction-free mode and a powerful search functionality.

Atom, created by GitHub, is an open-source editor with a strong emphasis on community-driven development and customization. Each of these tools has its own strengths, and the choice may depend on factors such as project complexity, personal workflow, and preferred features.

Regardless of the development environment chosen, configuring it properly is crucial for an efficient coding workflow. This includes setting up a Python interpreter, configuring project settings, and installing any necessary plugins or extensions. The Python interpreter is the engine that executes Python code, and ensuring that your IDE or editor is linked to the correct interpreter is essential. Most modern IDEs and editors offer options to specify the path to the Python interpreter, which allows you to manage multiple Python versions and virtual environments seamlessly.

Once your development environment is set up, running your first Python script is a significant milestone. This process begins with creating a new file in your IDE or editor and saving it with a `.py` extension, which indicates that it is a Python script. The content of the script can be as simple as a single line of code. For example, typing `print("Hello, world!")` is a classic introductory exercise in Python programming. This line of code utilizes the `print` function, which outputs the specified text to the console. Running this script involves executing the file through your IDE or editor's built-in functionality or using the command line.

To execute a Python script from the command line, navigate to the directory containing the script file and use the command `python scriptname.py`, where `scriptname.py` is the name of your Python file. This command invokes the Python interpreter to execute the script. Upon successful execution, the text "Hello, world!" should appear in the console, confirming that the script ran correctly. This simple exercise not only demonstrates the basic functionality of Python but also provides a foundation for more complex programming tasks.

The ability to run scripts and observe immediate results is a powerful feature of Python, which facilitates rapid development and testing. As you progress in your learning journey, you will encounter more sophisticated concepts and tools, but the fundamental process of writing, executing, and debugging Python code remains central to the programming experience.

In summary, the initial steps of exploring Python involve understanding its historical development and design principles, installing the language on various operating systems, setting up an effective development environment, and running your first script. Each of these steps builds upon the previous one, creating a solid foundation for further exploration of Python's features and capabilities. By familiarizing yourself with these aspects, you prepare yourself to tackle more advanced topics and projects with confidence and competence. As you continue to engage with Python, the skills and knowledge acquired through these early stages will serve as a valuable basis for your growth as a programmer.

CHAPTER 2:

Python's flexibility in handling different data types is further exemplified by its support for type conversion, a crucial aspect of working with data. Type conversion refers to the process of converting one data type into another. This is often necessary when performing operations that involve mixed data types or when data needs to be transformed to fit specific requirements.

Implicit type conversion, also known as automatic type conversion, occurs when Python automatically converts one data type to another during an operation. For example, if an integer and a float are used in a mathematical operation, Python implicitly converts the integer to a float before performing the operation. Consider the expression `5 + 3.2`. Python converts the integer `5` to a float, resulting in the float `5.0`, and then performs the addition, yielding `8.2`. This automatic handling of different data types simplifies code and reduces the need for explicit conversion in many cases.

Explicit type conversion, on the other hand, involves manually converting data from one type to another using specific functions. Python provides several built-in functions for this purpose. The `int()` function converts a value to an integer, `float()` converts a value to a floating-point number, and `str()` converts a value to a string. For instance, if we have a float value `7.5` and want to convert it to an integer, we can use `int(7.5)`, which will yield `7` by truncating the decimal part. Similarly, converting the integer `4` to a string using `str(4)` will result in the string `'4'`.

Another important aspect of Python's data handling is its

dynamic typing system. Unlike statically typed languages where variables must be declared with a specific type, Python allows variables to be assigned and reassigned values of different types without explicit type declarations. This dynamic typing simplifies coding and enhances flexibility, as it enables the same variable to be used with various types of data throughout a program. For example, a variable `data` can initially hold an integer value such as `10`, and later be reassigned to a string like `"Hello"`. Python's dynamic typing automatically adjusts the type of `data` based on the assigned value.

Understanding Python's syntax rules and conventions is essential for writing clear and effective code. Python's syntax emphasizes readability and simplicity, making it a popular choice for both beginners and experienced programmers. One fundamental syntax rule is the use of indentation to define code blocks. Unlike many other programming languages that use braces or keywords to delimit blocks of code, Python relies on indentation to indicate the beginning and end of blocks. This approach not only enforces a consistent style but also enhances code readability. For instance, in a conditional statement, the code inside the `if` block must be indented, typically by four spaces:

```python
if x > 10:
    print("x is greater than 10")
```

The consistency of indentation in Python is not merely a stylistic choice but a syntactic requirement. Incorrect indentation will lead to syntax errors, which can be identified and corrected by ensuring that all code blocks are properly aligned.

Python also uses the concept of comments to provide explanations or notes within the code. Comments are ignored by the interpreter and are intended solely for human readers. Single-line comments begin with the hash symbol (` `), while multi-line comments can be enclosed in triple quotes (`'''` or `"""`). For example:

```python
This is a single-line comment

"""
This is a
multi-line comment
"""
```

Comments are invaluable for documenting code, making it easier to understand and maintain.

When working with strings, Python provides a range of methods and operations to manipulate and analyze text. String concatenation, for instance, involves joining two or more strings together using the `+` operator. To combine the strings `"Hello"` and `"World"`, one would write `"Hello" + " " + "World"`, resulting in the string `"Hello World"`. String slicing allows for extracting a portion of a string by specifying a range of indices. For example, `"Python"[1:4]` yields `"yth"`, which represents the substring from index 1 to 3.

Another useful feature of Python's string handling is the ability to format strings. String formatting enables the inclusion of variable values within a string in a readable and concise manner. Python offers several methods for formatting, including the use of f-strings (formatted string literals) introduced in Python 3.6. An f-string is created by prefixing a string literal with the letter `f` and allows for the embedding of expressions inside curly braces `{}`. For example, `name "Alice"` and `f"Hello, {name}!"` evaluates to `"Hello, Alice!"`.

By mastering these fundamental aspects of Python's syntax

and data types, you lay a solid foundation for more advanced programming concepts. The ability to effectively utilize variables, operators, and data types, combined with an understanding of type conversion and dynamic typing, equips you with the skills necessary to tackle increasingly complex programming challenges.

The elegance of Python's syntax is further highlighted through its use of operators, which are integral to performing various operations on data. Operators in Python are symbols that represent computations or manipulations performed on variables and values. The basic operators include arithmetic operators, comparison operators, logical operators, and assignment operators, each serving distinct purposes.

Arithmetic operators are used to perform mathematical calculations. Python supports a range of arithmetic operators, including addition (`+`), subtraction (`-`), multiplication (` `), division (`/`), integer division (`//`), modulus (`%`), and exponentiation (` `). For example, the expression `7 + 3` evaluates to `10`, while `10 / 3` results in approximately `3.3333`. Integer division with `//` yields the quotient without the remainder, so `10 // 3` results in `3`. The modulus operator (`%`) returns the remainder of a division operation, such as `10 % 3`, which yields `1`. Exponentiation, denoted by ` `, calculates the power of a number, as in `2 3`, which results in `8`.

Comparison operators are used to compare values and return boolean results. These operators include equality (` `), inequality (`!`), greater than (`>`), less than (`<`), greater than or equal to (`>`), and less than or equal to (`<`). For instance, the expression `5 5` evaluates to `True`, while `5 ! 3` yields `True`. Comparison operators are essential in control flow statements, allowing programs to make decisions based on conditions.

Logical operators are used to combine multiple boolean

10

expressions or conditions. The primary logical operators in Python are `and`, `or`, and `not`. The `and` operator returns `True` only if both conditions are `True`. For example, `True and False` results in `False`. The `or` operator returns `True` if at least one of the conditions is `True`, so `True or False` evaluates to `True`. The `not` operator negates a boolean value, meaning `not True` yields `False`. Logical operators are particularly useful in conditional statements and loops, where multiple conditions need to be evaluated together.

Assignment operators are used to assign values to variables and can also perform operations during the assignment. The basic assignment operator is ` `, which assigns a value to a variable. For example, `x 10` assigns the value `10` to the variable `x`. In addition to the basic assignment, Python includes compound assignment operators that combine arithmetic operations with assignment. These include `+`, `-`, ` `, `/`, `//`, `%` and ` `. For instance, `x + 5` is shorthand for `x x + 5`, which increments the value of `x` by `5`. Similarly, `x 2` multiplies the current value of `x` by `2` and assigns the result back to `x`.

Understanding the role of comments in Python is also crucial for writing maintainable code. Comments are notes embedded within code to explain or clarify sections for human readers. They are ignored by the Python interpreter and do not affect the execution of the program. In Python, comments are indicated by the hash symbol (` `). Any text following a ` ` on the same line is treated as a comment. For example, ` This is a comment` is ignored by the interpreter. Comments are especially useful for documenting the purpose of code sections, explaining complex logic, or noting any potential issues.

String manipulation and formatting are additional areas where Python's syntax proves to be both versatile and user-friendly. Strings in Python support a wide range of methods for modification and formatting. The `str` type includes methods like `upper()`, `lower()`, `strip()`, `replace()`, and `split()`. The `upper()` method converts all characters in a string to uppercase, while `lower()` converts them to lowercase. The `strip()` method removes any leading or trailing whitespace from a string. The `replace()` method replaces specified substrings with new ones, and `split()` divides a string into a list based on a specified delimiter.

String formatting allows for the dynamic insertion of values into strings, making it possible to create formatted output. Python offers several approaches to string formatting, including the `format()` method and f-strings (formatted string literals). The `format()` method uses curly braces `{}` as placeholders within a string, which are then replaced with values provided as arguments to the `format()` method. For instance, `'Hello, {}'.format('world')` results in `'Hello, world'`. F-strings, introduced in Python 3.6, provide a more concise and readable way to format strings by prefixing the string with an `f` and including expressions inside curly braces. For example, `f'Hello, {name}'` will embed the value of the variable `name` into the string.

Mastering these fundamental aspects of Python syntax and data types is essential for building a solid foundation in programming. By understanding how to declare variables, use operators, and manipulate different data types, you lay the groundwork for more advanced programming concepts and techniques. Python's emphasis on readability and simplicity helps ensure that even complex code remains understandable and maintainable, fostering a productive and efficient programming environment.

CHAPTER 3:

The `for` loop in Python is designed to iterate over a sequence of elements, such as items in a list, characters in a string, or values in a range. It is particularly useful when you need to execute a block of code for each item in a collection. The syntax for a `for` loop is straightforward:

```python
for item in sequence:
    code to execute
```

Here, `sequence` represents the collection of items to iterate over, and `item` is a variable that takes on the value of each element in the sequence during each iteration. For example, consider a list of numbers and a `for` loop that prints each number:

```python
numbers [1, 2, 3, 4, 5]
for number in numbers:
   print(number)
```

In this case, the `for` loop iterates over the `numbers` list, with the variable `number` taking on the value of each element in turn. The `print` statement outputs each number, resulting in the sequence `1 2 3 4 5` being printed to the console.

The `range()` function is often used in conjunction with `for` loops to generate a sequence of numbers. The `range()` function can take one, two, or three arguments: the start value, the stop value, and the step value. For instance:

```python
for i in range(5):
    print(i)
```

This loop will output the numbers `0` through `4`, as `range(5)` generates a sequence from `0` to `4`. If you need a different starting point or step size, you can provide additional arguments. For example, `range(2, 10, 2)` generates the sequence `2, 4, 6, 8`.

The `while` loop provides a mechanism for repeated execution based on a condition. Unlike the `for` loop, which iterates over a sequence, the `while` loop continues to execute as long as its condition evaluates to `True`. The syntax for a `while` loop is as follows:

```python
while condition:
    code to execute
```

The `condition` is an expression that is evaluated before each iteration. As long as this condition remains `True`, the code block within the `while` loop will continue to execute. It is crucial to ensure that the condition eventually becomes `False` to avoid creating an infinite loop. Consider a `while` loop that prints numbers from `0` to `4`:

```python
i 0
while i < 5:
    print(i)
    i + 1
```

In this example, the loop starts with `i` set to `0`. It prints the value of `i` and then increments `i` by `1`. The loop continues as long as `i` is less than `5`. Once `i` reaches `5`, the condition `i < 5` becomes `False`, and the loop terminates.

In addition to these basic control flow mechanisms, functions are a cornerstone of Python programming. Functions allow you to encapsulate code into reusable blocks, making programs more modular and manageable. Defining a function in Python involves using the `def` keyword, followed by the function name and a set of parentheses that may include parameters. The function body is indented and contains the code to execute when the function is called. For example:

```python
def greet(name):
    print(f"Hello, {name}!")
```

In this function, `greet`, the parameter `name` is used to personalize the greeting message. When `greet("Alice")` is called, the function prints "Hello, Alice!" to the console.

Functions can also return values using the `return` statement. This allows a function to produce a result that can be used elsewhere in the program. For instance:

```python
def add(a, b):
    return a + b
```

The `add` function takes two parameters, `a` and `b`, and returns their sum. Calling `add(3, 4)` returns `7`, which can be assigned to a variable or used directly in expressions.

It is also possible to define functions with default parameter values. This feature provides flexibility by allowing arguments to be omitted when calling the function, as the default values will be used instead. For example:

```python
def greet(name"Guest"):
    print(f"Hello, {name}!")
```

In this function, if no argument is provided for `name`, it defaults to `"Guest"`. Calling `greet()` results in "Hello, Guest!", while `greet("Alice")` produces "Hello, Alice!".

In summary, mastering control flow constructs and functions is essential for writing efficient and reusable Python code. Conditional statements allow for decision-making based on conditions, while looping constructs enable repetitive actions. Functions further enhance code organization by encapsulating tasks into modular units, supporting parameters, and returning values. Understanding and applying these concepts will provide a solid foundation for more complex programming tasks and algorithm development.

The `while` loop provides a mechanism for repeated execution based on a condition. Unlike the `for` loop, which iterates over a sequence, the `while` loop continues to execute as long as its condition evaluates to `True`. The syntax for a `while` loop is as follows:

```python
while condition:
    code to execute
```

The `condition` is an expression that is evaluated before each iteration. As long as this condition remains `True`, the loop executes the associated block of code. If the condition becomes `False`, the loop terminates. For instance, the following code snippet demonstrates a `while` loop that counts down from `5` to `1`:

```python
```

```
count 5
while count > 0:
  print(count)
  count - 1
```

Here, the `while` loop continues as long as `count` is greater than `0`. Within the loop, `count` is printed and then decremented by `1` on each iteration. Once `count` reaches `0`, the condition `count > 0` becomes `False`, and the loop terminates, producing the output `5 4 3 2 1`.

It is crucial to ensure that the condition in a `while` loop will eventually become `False`; otherwise, the loop will result in an infinite loop, which can cause a program to hang or crash. To avoid such scenarios, ensure that the loop's condition is updated in a way that it will eventually be met.

Functions are a cornerstone of modular and reusable programming. They allow you to encapsulate a block of code into a single, reusable entity. Functions can be defined using the `def` keyword followed by the function name, a pair of parentheses, and a colon. The body of the function is indented under the function definition. Here is an example of a simple function that adds two numbers:

```python
def add_numbers(a, b):
  return a + b
```

In this function, `add_numbers`, two parameters `a` and `b` are defined. The `return` statement specifies the value to be returned to the caller. When this function is called with specific arguments, it computes the sum of `a` and `b` and returns the result.

Functions can also have default parameter values, which

provide a way to specify default arguments if none are provided by the caller. For instance:

```python
def greet(name"Guest"):
    print(f"Hello, {name}!")
```

In this function, `name` has a default value of `"Guest"`. If no argument is provided when calling `greet()`, it will use this default value. However, if an argument is provided, such as `greet("Alice")`, it will override the default, resulting in the output "Hello, Alice!".

Additionally, functions can accept a variable number of arguments using `args` and `kwargs`. The `args` syntax allows a function to accept any number of positional arguments, which are received as a tuple within the function. For example:

```python
def sum_numbers(args):
    return sum(args)
```

Calling `sum_numbers(1, 2, 3, 4)` will return `10` because `args` is a tuple containing all the provided arguments, which are then summed up.

Similarly, `kwargs` allows a function to accept any number of keyword arguments, which are received as a dictionary. This is useful for functions that need to handle named arguments flexibly. For example:

```python
def print_info(kwargs):
    for key, value in kwargs.items():
        print(f"{key}: {value}")
```

Calling `print_info(name"Alice", age30)` will output:

```
name: Alice
age: 30
```

This approach allows for dynamic and flexible argument handling.

Encapsulating logic within functions not only improves code readability but also enhances maintainability and reusability. Functions enable you to break down complex problems into smaller, manageable parts, each responsible for a specific task. By defining functions, you can avoid code duplication and make your codebase easier to understand and modify.

The integration of control flow mechanisms and functions provides a powerful toolkit for developing more sophisticated and efficient programs. Conditional statements and loops offer the means to handle various execution paths and repetitive tasks, while functions allow for organized and modular code design. Mastering these concepts is essential for advancing in Python programming and tackling more complex challenges.

CHAPTER 4:

Lists also provide methods to insert and remove elements at specific positions. The `insert()` method allows you to add an element at a particular index, shifting subsequent elements to the right. For example:

```python
numbers.insert(2, 10)
```

This inserts the value `10` at index `2`, resulting in the list `[1, 2, 10, 3, 4, 5]`. Conversely, the `remove()` method removes the first occurrence of a specified value:

```python
numbers.remove(10)
```

This removes the first instance of `10`, reverting the list to `[1, 2, 3, 4, 5]`. If an element does not exist in the list, using `remove()` will raise a `ValueError`. To handle this, you can use a conditional check before removal or use the `pop()` method, which removes an element at a specified index and returns it. For instance:

```python
removed_element numbers.pop(1)
```

This removes and returns the element at index `1`, which is `2`, leaving the list `[1, 3, 4, 5]`.

Lists are particularly useful when you need a collection of items that may change over time. However, when immutability is desired or required, tuples offer a robust alternative. Unlike lists, tuples are immutable, meaning their contents cannot be altered after creation. This immutability provides several advantages, such as ensuring data integrity and allowing tuples to be used as keys in dictionaries or elements in sets, where mutable types cannot be used.

Tuples are defined using parentheses `()`, with elements separated by commas. For example, a tuple containing three elements can be defined as:

```python
coordinates (10, 20, 30)
```

Accessing elements in a tuple is similar to lists, using indexing. For instance, `coordinates[1]` returns `20`. Slicing in tuples follows the same syntax as with lists, allowing you to extract portions of a tuple:

```python
subset coordinates[1:]
```

This extracts the elements from index `1` to the end, resulting in `(20, 30)`.

Since tuples are immutable, they do not support methods that modify their content. There are no `append()`, `insert()`, or `remove()` methods for tuples. Instead, if you need to create a new tuple with additional elements, you must concatenate tuples. For instance:

```python
extended_coordinates coordinates + (40, 50)
```

This creates a new tuple `(10, 20, 30, 40, 50)`, combining the original tuple with additional values. Similarly, if you want to repeat a tuple's elements, you can use the repetition operator ```:

```python
repeated_coordinates coordinates 2
```

This results in `(10, 20, 30, 10, 20, 30)`.

Understanding the distinctions between lists and tuples helps in choosing the appropriate data structure for your needs. Lists are ideal for collections of items that may need to be modified, whereas tuples are suitable for fixed collections where immutability is beneficial. By leveraging these data structures effectively, you can write more efficient and reliable Python programs.

When working with lists and tuples, consider their performance implications. Lists, due to their mutable nature, involve additional overhead for operations that modify their content. Tuples, being immutable, offer faster access times and lower memory overhead, which can be advantageous in performance-critical applications.

To summarize, mastering lists and tuples is fundamental to Python programming. Lists provide a versatile and dynamic way to manage collections of items, while tuples offer a fixed, immutable alternative. Both data structures come with their own set of operations and use cases, and understanding these nuances allows you to select the right data structure based on your program's requirements.

Tuples are also utilized for grouping data in a way that reflects a structured collection. For example, they are commonly used to represent records where each element holds a distinct piece of information. Consider a scenario where you need to store information about a book, including its title, author, and publication year. A tuple provides a convenient way to bundle these attributes together:

```python
book ("The Great Gatsby", "F. Scott Fitzgerald", 1925)
```

In this tuple, `book[0]` retrieves the title, `book[1]` retrieves the author, and `book[2]` retrieves the publication year. The immutability of tuples ensures that these values cannot be inadvertently altered, thus preserving the integrity of the data.

When deciding between lists and tuples, several factors come into play. Lists are preferred when you need a collection of items that can be modified, as they support operations such as appending, removing, and altering elements. They are ideal for use cases where the data is expected to change over time, such as maintaining a dynamic list of user inputs or managing a collection of items in a shopping cart.

On the other hand, tuples are chosen for their immutability, which provides several advantages in specific contexts. For instance, tuples can be used as keys in dictionaries or elements in sets because their immutable nature ensures that their hash value remains constant, making them suitable for these data structures where the keys or elements must be unchanging. Additionally, tuples are more memory efficient than lists, as their fixed size and immutability allow Python to optimize their storage and access.

To further illustrate the usage of these data structures, let us explore a practical example involving both lists and tuples. Suppose you are developing a program to track students' grades. You might use a list to maintain a collection of student records, where each record is a tuple containing the student's name, ID, and grade. This setup allows you to easily manage and update the list of students while keeping each student's data immutable within the tuple.

Here's how you might implement this:

```python
students [
  ("Alice", 101, 85),
  ("Bob", 102, 90),
  ("Charlie", 103, 78)
]
```

To update Bob's grade, you would first need to locate his record in the list, modify the grade, and then reconstruct the tuple with the updated information. For example:

```python
students[1] ("Bob", 102, 92)  Update Bob's grade to 92
```

The list of students now contains the updated record with Bob's new grade. This example demonstrates how lists and tuples can be effectively used together to manage collections of immutable data within a mutable container.

Understanding when to use each data structure is crucial for effective programming in Python. Lists and tuples each serve unique purposes, and choosing the appropriate one for a given task can significantly impact the performance and maintainability of your code. By mastering these fundamental data structures, you gain the ability to handle a wide range of programming challenges efficiently and elegantly.

In summary, lists and tuples are foundational data structures in Python that provide powerful mechanisms for organizing and managing data. Lists offer flexibility with mutable elements and a wide range of operations, making them suitable for dynamic collections of items. Tuples, with their immutability, provide a way to group related data in a fixed and reliable manner. By understanding their characteristics and use cases, you will be equipped to select the most appropriate data structure for your programming needs.

CHAPTER 5:

To delete an entry from a dictionary, you can use the `del` statement followed by the key of the entry you wish to remove:

```python
del student_grades["Charlie"]
```

This removes the key-value pair associated with the key `"Charlie"`, resulting in a dictionary that now only contains `"Alice"`, `"Bob"`, and `"David"`. Alternatively, the `pop()` method can be used, which not only removes the specified key but also returns its value:

```python
removed_grade student_grades.pop("Alice")
```

This removes `"Alice"` from the dictionary and assigns `85` to `removed_grade`. If the key does not exist, `pop()` raises a `KeyError` unless a default value is provided as a second argument:

```python
removed_grade student_grades.pop("Eve", "Not Found")
```

This returns `"Not Found"` if `"Eve"` is not a key in the dictionary.

Dictionaries also provide methods to view their keys, values, and key-value pairs. The `keys()` method returns a view object of the dictionary's keys, while `values()` returns a view object of the values. To view both keys and values together, you can use the `items()` method:

```python
keys student_grades.keys()
values student_grades.values()
items student_grades.items()
```

These methods return view objects, which reflect changes made to the dictionary. For example, if you add a new entry to `student_grades`, the view objects `keys`, `values`, and `items` will include the new entry.

Sets, on the other hand, are another fundamental data structure in Python that provides a collection of unique items. Unlike lists or dictionaries, sets do not store items in a specific order, and duplicate elements are automatically removed. This makes sets particularly useful for membership testing, removing duplicates, and performing mathematical set operations such as union, intersection, and difference.

To create a set, you use curly braces `{}` or the `set()` constructor. Here is an example using curly braces:

```python
fruits {"apple", "banana", "cherry"}
```

Sets created with curly braces cannot contain duplicate elements. If you attempt to add a duplicate element, the set will remain unchanged:

```python
fruits.add("apple")
```

The set `fruits` still remains `{"apple", "banana", "cherry"}`. To remove an element from a set, you can use the `remove()`

method, which raises a `KeyError` if the element is not found:

```python
fruits.remove("banana")
```

Alternatively, the `discard()` method can be used, which does not raise an error if the element is not found:

```python
fruits.discard("banana")
```

To remove and return an arbitrary element, you can use the `pop()` method. This method is particularly useful when you need to process and remove items from a set:

```python
element fruits.pop()
```

The `pop()` method removes and returns an arbitrary element from the set, and if the set is empty, it raises a `KeyError`.

Sets support several mathematical operations that are particularly useful in various applications. For instance, the union of two sets combines all unique elements from both sets. You can compute the union using the `|` operator or the `union()` method:

```python
set1 {1, 2, 3}
set2 {3, 4, 5}
union_set set1 | set2
```

The resulting set `union_set` will be `{1, 2, 3, 4, 5}`. Similarly, the intersection of two sets provides a set containing only elements that are present in both sets. This can be computed using the `&` operator or the `intersection()` method:

```python
intersection_set  set1 & set2
```

The resulting set `intersection_set` will be `{3}`. The difference between two sets yields a set containing elements that are in the first set but not in the second set, which can be computed using the `-` operator or the `difference()` method:

```python
difference_set  set1 - set2
```

The resulting set `difference_set` will be `{1, 2}`. Additionally, the symmetric difference between two sets provides a set of elements that are in either of the sets but not in both. This can be computed using the `^` operator or the `symmetric_difference()` method:

```python
symmetric_difference_set  set1 ^ set2
```

The resulting set `symmetric_difference_set` will be `{1, 2, 4, 5}`.

By mastering these operations and understanding when to use dictionaries versus sets, you can efficiently manage and manipulate data in your Python programs, ensuring that you make the most of Python's powerful data structures.

To demonstrate how sets handle duplicates, consider the following example:

```python
fruits  {"apple", "banana", "cherry"}
fruits.add("banana")
```

In this case, adding `"banana"` again to the `fruits` set has no effect, as sets automatically discard duplicate elements. This characteristic is particularly valuable when you need to ensure that a collection contains only unique items.

The `remove()` method can be used to delete a specific element from a set. If the element is not present, `remove()` will raise a `KeyError`. For example:

```python
fruits.remove("cherry")
```

This statement removes `"cherry"` from the set. If you attempt to remove an element not in the set, a `KeyError` will be raised. Alternatively, the `discard()` method can be used, which will not raise an error if the element is absent:

```python
fruits.discard("grape")
```

Here, `"grape"` is not in the set, but no error occurs. This method is useful when you want to remove an item if it exists, but do not want to handle potential errors if it does not.

To clear all elements from a set, you can use the `clear()` method:

```python
fruits.clear()
```

This empties the set, leaving it with no elements. The `pop()` method, on the other hand, removes and returns an arbitrary element from the set. Since sets are unordered, you cannot predict which element will be removed:

```python
```

element fruits.pop()
```

The `pop()` method is particularly useful in scenarios where you need to retrieve and remove an element from a set without caring which one is chosen.

Sets also support various mathematical set operations, which are useful for comparing and combining sets of data. The union operation, represented by the `|` operator or the `union()` method, combines all elements from two sets, removing any duplicates:

```python
set1 {"apple", "banana", "cherry"}
set2 {"banana", "cherry", "date"}
union_set set1 | set2
```

The `union_set` will contain `{"apple", "banana", "cherry", "date"}`. Alternatively, you can use the `union()` method:

```python
union_set set1.union(set2)
```

Intersection, represented by the `&` operator or the `intersection()` method, yields only the elements that are present in both sets:

```python
intersection_set set1 & set2
```

The `intersection_set` will contain `{"banana", "cherry"}`. The `intersection()` method provides the same result:

```python
intersection_set set1.intersection(set2)
```
```

Difference, indicated by the `-` operator or the `difference()` method, provides the elements that are in the first set but not in the second:

```python
difference_set set1 - set2
```

This will result in `{"apple"}`. The `difference()` method yields the same result:

```python
difference_set set1.difference(set2)
```

Symmetric difference, represented by the `^` operator or the `symmetric_difference()` method, yields elements that are in either set but not in both:

```python
symmetric_difference_set set1 ^ set2
```

The result will be `{"apple", "date"}`. Using the `symmetric_difference()` method will yield the same outcome:

```python
symmetric_difference_set set1.symmetric_difference(set2)
```

Understanding and utilizing these operations can greatly enhance your ability to manage and analyze data efficiently. Both dictionaries and sets offer unique advantages for different types of tasks, and mastering their functionalities will significantly improve your programming proficiency.

In summary, dictionaries and sets are foundational data structures in Python that provide powerful methods for managing collections of data. Dictionaries allow for efficient data retrieval and modification using key-value pairs, while sets offer unique collections with capabilities for mathematical set operations. By effectively leveraging these data structures, you can handle complex data management tasks with ease and efficiency.

CHAPTER 6:

When it comes to writing data to a file, Python offers several methods for this operation, depending on the file mode used. If a file is opened in write mode (`'w'`), any existing content is overwritten. To write a string to the file, the `write()` method is employed:

```python
file open('example.txt', 'w')
file.write('Hello, World!')
file.close()
```

In this example, the file `example.txt` is opened, the string `'Hello, World!'` is written to it, and then the file is closed. Closing the file is crucial as it ensures that all data is properly saved and that system resources are released.

For appending data to a file without removing its existing content, the append mode (`'a'`) should be used:

```python
file open('example.txt', 'a')
file.write('Appending new content.\n')
file.close()
```

This operation will add `'Appending new content.'` at the end of the existing file content. The newline character (`'\n'`) is used to ensure that the new content appears on a new line.

When working with binary files, such as images or executable files, it's essential to open the file in binary mode by appending a `'b'` to the mode string. For example, to read a binary file:

```python
file open('image.jpg', 'rb')
binary_data file.read()
file.close()
```

Here, `'rb'` opens the file in read-binary mode, and `file.read()` retrieves the binary data.

Similarly, writing binary data involves:

```python
file open('image_copy.jpg', 'wb')
file.write(binary_data)
file.close()
```

In this case, `'wb'` opens the file in write-binary mode, and the binary data is written to `image_copy.jpg`.

It is important to handle errors that may occur during file operations. For instance, trying to open a file that does not exist in read mode will result in a `FileNotFoundError`. To manage such scenarios gracefully, use exception handling with `try` and `except` blocks:

```python
try:
   file open('nonexistent.txt', 'r')
   content file.read()
except FileNotFoundError:
   print("The file was not found.")
finally:
   file.close()
```

In this code, if the file is not found, a message is printed, and the `finally` block ensures that the file is closed if it was successfully opened. This practice prevents potential resource leaks.

User input and output operations in Python are handled using the `input()` and `print()` functions, respectively. The `input()` function reads a line of text from the user and returns it as a string:

```python
user_name input("Enter your name: ")
```

This statement prompts the user to enter their name and stores it in the variable `user_name`. You can then use this data in your program. For example, to greet the user:

```python
print(f"Hello, {user_name}!")
```

The `print()` function outputs data to the console. It can handle multiple arguments, separating them by spaces, and allows for formatted output using f-strings or other formatting techniques.

Python also supports formatted strings, which enable more complex output formatting. Using f-strings (formatted string literals), you can embed expressions inside string literals for more readable and concise code:

```python
age 25
print(f"You are {age} years old.")
```

This will output: `"You are 25 years old."`

Alternatively, the `format()` method offers another way to format strings:

```python
print("You are {} years old.".format(age))
```

This method replaces the curly braces `{}` with the value of `age`. Both f-strings and `format()` can be used to control the output format, including padding, alignment, and precision.

Handling user input and managing file operations effectively are crucial skills in programming. By understanding these processes, you can build robust applications that interact with users and handle data efficiently.

Handling user input and output in Python involves using the `input()` function to gather data from the user and the `print()` function to display information to the console. These functions are fundamental for creating interactive programs.

The `input()` function reads a line of text from the user and returns it as a string. For example:

```python
name input("Enter your name: ")
print("Hello, " + name + "!")
```

In this snippet, the `input()` function prompts the user to enter their name. The entered value is stored in the variable `name`, which is then used in a greeting message printed to the console. It is important to note that `input()` always returns data as a string, regardless of the actual content entered. To work with different data types, such as integers or floats, you must explicitly convert the input:

```python
age int(input("Enter your age: "))
```

```
print("You are " + str(age) + " years old.")
```

Here, `int()` converts the input string to an integer. If the input cannot be converted (e.g., if the user types non-numeric characters), Python will raise a `ValueError`. To handle such errors, consider using exception handling:

```python
try:
    age int(input("Enter your age: "))
    print("You are " + str(age) + " years old.")
except ValueError:
    print("Please enter a valid number.")
```

This approach ensures that the program does not crash and provides the user with a prompt to enter a valid number.

For outputting data, the `print()` function is quite versatile. It can handle multiple arguments and automatically separates them with spaces by default:

```python
print("Name:", name, "Age:", age)
```

You can also format output using f-strings, which provide a more readable and concise way to embed expressions inside string literals:

```python
print(f"Name: {name}, Age: {age}")
```

F-strings evaluate expressions at runtime and can include various formatting options. For example, to format a floating-point number to two decimal places:

```python
```

```
pi 3.141592653589793
print(f"Value of pi: {pi:.2f}")
```

This will output `Value of pi: 3.14`, rounding the value to two decimal places.

When dealing with files and user input, it is often useful to combine these elements. For instance, a common task might involve writing user input to a file:

```python
filename input("Enter the filename to save: ")
with open(filename, 'w') as file:
    content input("Enter the content to write to the file: ")
    file.write(content)
```

In this code, the filename is provided by the user, and the content to be written is also collected via `input()`. The `with` statement ensures that the file is properly closed after the block is executed, even if an error occurs.

Similarly, reading from a file and processing its contents can involve user input:

```python
filename input("Enter the filename to read: ")
try:
    with open(filename, 'r') as file:
        content file.read()
        print("File content:\n" + content)
except FileNotFoundError:
    print("The file was not found.")
```

Here, the program prompts the user for a filename, attempts to read the file, and displays its contents. If the file does not exist, an appropriate error message is shown.

Combining file handling with user input and output allows for the creation of interactive and dynamic programs. By understanding and applying these concepts, you can effectively manage data and create robust applications that handle user interactions and data persistence efficiently.

CHAPTER 7:

When it comes to handling exceptions in Python, the `finally` block plays a crucial role. Regardless of whether an exception was raised or not, the `finally` block is executed. This block is typically used for clean-up actions that must be performed under all circumstances, such as closing a file or releasing resources.

Consider the following example where a file is opened for reading:

```python
try:
  file open('example.txt', 'r')
  data file.read()
   Potentially problematic code
except FileNotFoundError:
  print("The file was not found.")
finally:
  file.close()
  print("File closed.")
```

In this code, the `finally` block ensures that the file is closed, even if an exception occurs while reading the file. This prevents resource leakage and ensures that the file handle is properly released.

The `else` block, when used in conjunction with `try` and `except`, executes if no exceptions are raised in the `try` block. This is useful for code that should only run when the `try` block succeeds without issues:

```python
try:
    value int(input("Enter a number: "))
    result 10 / value
except ZeroDivisionError:
    print("Division by zero is not allowed.")
except ValueError:
    print("Please enter a valid number.")
else:
    print(f"The result is {result}.")
finally:
    print("Execution completed.")
```

In this example, if the user inputs a valid number that is not zero, the `else` block will execute, displaying the result. Regardless of the outcome, the `finally` block will run, indicating the end of the execution.

Understanding the common exceptions that might occur is vital for effective error handling. Python includes numerous built-in exceptions, each representing a specific type of error. Common exceptions include `IndexError` for accessing an invalid index in a list, `KeyError` for accessing a non-existent key in a dictionary, and `TypeError` for operations or functions applied to inappropriate data types.

Here's an example illustrating `IndexError`:

```python
my_list [1, 2, 3]
try:
    print(my_list[5])
except IndexError:
    print("Index out of range.")
```

In this snippet, trying to access an index that doesn't exist triggers an `IndexError`, which is then handled by the `except` block.

Creating custom exceptions allows you to handle specific scenarios that aren't covered by built-in exceptions. You achieve this by defining a new exception class that inherits from Python's built-in `Exception` class. For instance:

```python
class NegativeValueError(Exception):
    def __init__(self, message"Value cannot be negative"):
        self.message message
        super().__init__(self.message)

def process_value(value):
    if value < 0:
        raise NegativeValueError("Negative value provided.")
    return value 2

try:
    result process_value(-5)
except NegativeValueError as e:
    print(e)
```

In this example, `NegativeValueError` is a custom exception used to indicate that a negative value is invalid. The `process_value` function raises this exception if the input value is negative, and it is caught and handled in the `try` block.

Exception handling not only allows you to manage errors effectively but also contributes to better code organization and readability. By using specific `except` blocks for different exceptions, you can provide more precise error messages and handling strategies. The `finally` and `else` blocks further enhance the robustness of your code by ensuring essential clean-up actions and executing code that should run only on successful completion of the `try` block.

In practice, effective exception handling is crucial for developing reliable and user-friendly applications. It enables your programs to handle unexpected situations gracefully, preventing crashes and ensuring that resources are properly managed. Mastering these concepts will allow you to build more resilient Python applications and handle errors with confidence.

When designing error-handling mechanisms, it's also crucial to understand how to create custom exceptions to manage specific error scenarios. Custom exceptions are particularly useful when the built-in exceptions do not provide enough detail for the error context. By defining your own exception classes, you can provide more meaningful error messages and handle exceptions in a way that fits your application's needs.

To create a custom exception, you typically define a new class that inherits from Python's built-in `Exception` class. Here's a step-by-step process to define and use a custom exception:

First, define the custom exception class. This class should inherit from the `Exception` class and, optionally, override the `__init__` method to customize the error message:

```python
class CustomError(Exception):
    def __init__(self, message):
        super().__init__(message)
        self.message = message
```

In this custom exception, `CustomError`, we have overridden the `__init__` method to accept a custom error message, which is then passed to the base `Exception` class.

Next, you can raise this custom exception in your code whenever a specific error condition is met. For instance, if you are building a function that expects a positive integer, you might raise a `CustomError` if the input is invalid:

```python
def process_number(value):
    if value < 0:
        raise CustomError("The value must be a positive integer.")
    Process the value
    print(f"Processing {value}...")

try:
    process_number(-5)
except CustomError as e:
    print(f"Custom error occurred: {e}")
```

In this example, if the `process_number` function receives a non-positive integer, it raises a `CustomError` with a descriptive message. The `try` block catches this exception, and the `except` block handles it, displaying the custom error message.

Additionally, you might encounter situations where you need to catch multiple exceptions in one `except` block. Python allows you to handle multiple exceptions simultaneously by grouping them in a tuple:

```python
try:
    Code that might raise multiple exceptions
    pass
except (TypeError, ValueError) as e:
    print(f"An error occurred: {e}")
```

Here, the `except` block will catch either a `TypeError` or a `ValueError`, allowing you to handle them with the same error-handling logic. This approach is particularly useful when multiple exceptions require similar handling, simplifying your code and avoiding redundancy.

It is also essential to manage exceptions effectively to ensure your application remains robust and user-friendly. This involves not only catching exceptions but also ensuring that the program can recover gracefully or provide meaningful feedback to the user. For instance, logging exceptions can be a crucial aspect of debugging and monitoring in production environments. Python's `logging` module provides a flexible framework for recording logs, including exception information:

```python
import logging

logging.basicConfig(filename'app.log', levellogging.ERROR)

try:
    Code that might fail
    pass
except Exception as e:
    logging.error("An error occurred", exc_infoTrue)
```

In this snippet, any exception that occurs will be logged to `app.log` with the traceback information, facilitating troubleshooting and maintenance.

Exception handling in Python is designed to be flexible and powerful, enabling developers to write code that can anticipate, catch, and handle errors gracefully. By understanding and utilizing `try`, `except`, `finally`, and `else` blocks, along with custom exceptions and logging practices, you can build robust applications that are resilient to errors and provide a better user experience.

CHAPTER 8:

In addition to encapsulation, inheritance is another cornerstone of object-oriented programming that enhances the flexibility and scalability of code. Inheritance allows one class to derive attributes and methods from another, creating a hierarchical relationship between classes. This mechanism promotes code reuse by enabling a new class to extend or modify the behavior of an existing class without altering the original class's code.

To illustrate inheritance, let us expand our example with a class hierarchy involving `Car` and `ElectricCar`. Suppose we want to introduce a specialized type of car that has additional attributes and methods related to its electric nature. Instead of redefining all the properties and methods of `Car`, we can create `ElectricCar` as a subclass of `Car`. This subclass will inherit all the properties and methods of the `Car` class and can add or override functionality as needed.

Here is how we define the `ElectricCar` class:

```python
class ElectricCar(Car):
    def __init__(self, make, model, year, battery_size75):
        super().__init__(make, model, year)
        self.battery_size battery_size

    def describe_battery(self):
        return f"This car has a {self.battery_size}-kWh battery."
```

In this example, `ElectricCar` inherits from `Car` using the syntax `class ElectricCar(Car):`. The `__init__` method of `ElectricCar` calls `super().__init__(make, model, year)` to invoke the constructor of the `Car` class, initializing the common attributes. The `ElectricCar` class also introduces a new attribute, `battery_size`, and a new method, `describe_battery`, which provides information specific to electric cars.

Creating an instance of `ElectricCar` works similarly to creating an instance of `Car`, but it includes the additional functionality provided by the subclass:

```python
my_electric_car ElectricCar("Tesla", "Model S", 2023, battery_size100)
print(my_electric_car.display_info())  Output: 2023 Tesla Model S
print(my_electric_car.describe_battery())  Output: This car has a 100-kWh battery.
```

This demonstrates how inheritance allows for the extension of functionality while maintaining a clear relationship between classes. The `ElectricCar` class is an example of how inheritance can be used to model specialized entities based on a more general class.

Encapsulation and inheritance are crucial in designing robust object-oriented systems, but polymorphism adds a layer of flexibility that enhances the power of OOP. Polymorphism allows objects of different classes to be treated as objects of a common superclass. The key to polymorphism is the concept of method overriding, where a subclass provides a specific implementation of a method that is already defined in its superclass. This enables a single interface to be used for different underlying forms (data types).

Consider a situation where we have a base class `Animal` with a method `make_sound`. We can define different subclasses like `Dog` and `Cat` that override the `make_sound` method to provide specific behaviors for each type of animal. Here's an example:

```python
class Animal:
  def make_sound(self):
    raise NotImplementedError("Subclasses must implement this method")

class Dog(Animal):
  def make_sound(self):
    return "Woof!"

class Cat(Animal):
  def make_sound(self):
    return "Meow!"
```

In this code, `Animal` is an abstract base class with a method `make_sound` that is intended to be overridden by subclasses. The `Dog` and `Cat` classes provide their specific implementations of `make_sound`. When we create instances of `Dog` and `Cat` and call their `make_sound` methods, each class produces its own unique output:

```python
animals [Dog(), Cat()]

for animal in animals:
  print(animal.make_sound())
```

This loop demonstrates polymorphism, where each `Animal` object is treated uniformly, but the specific implementation of `make_sound` is determined by the actual type of object at runtime. The result will be:

```
```

Woof!
Meow!
```

Polymorphism enhances the flexibility and extensibility of code by allowing methods to be implemented in multiple ways, depending on the class of the object invoking the method.

Together, encapsulation, inheritance, and polymorphism form the backbone of object-oriented programming in Python. By leveraging these principles, developers can create well-organized, modular, and maintainable code that accurately represents real-world systems and behaviors. The ability to model complex interactions and relationships through classes and objects not only facilitates effective code reuse but also fosters the development of scalable and adaptive software solutions.

Polymorphism is another vital principle of object-oriented programming that enhances flexibility and integration within the code. Polymorphism allows objects of different classes to be treated as objects of a common superclass, particularly when it comes to methods. This means that a single method can operate in different ways depending on the object that invokes it. In Python, polymorphism is achieved through method overriding and duck typing.

Method overriding is a direct application of polymorphism where a subclass provides a specific implementation of a method that is already defined in its superclass. This allows a subclass to modify or extend the behavior of a method inherited from its parent class. Consider the following example with our `Car` and `ElectricCar` classes:

```python
class Car:
    def start_engine(self):
        return "The engine starts with a roar."
```
```

```python
class ElectricCar(Car):
  def start_engine(self):
    return "The car starts silently with an electric motor."
```

Here, the `ElectricCar` class overrides the `start_engine` method from the `Car` class. When calling `start_engine` on an instance of `ElectricCar`, the specific implementation in `ElectricCar` is executed, whereas an instance of `Car` would use the original implementation. This allows objects to exhibit different behaviors while sharing a common interface.

Duck typing, a concept prevalent in Python, supports polymorphism by focusing on whether an object can perform the required behavior rather than its exact type. In Python, the emphasis is on whether an object implements the necessary methods and behaviors rather than whether it is an instance of a particular class. This allows for greater flexibility and the use of polymorphism in a more dynamic fashion. For instance, if we define a method that accepts any object with a `start_engine` method, it will work with both `Car` and `ElectricCar` objects:

```python
def test_start_engine(vehicle):
  print(vehicle.start_engine())

my_car Car()
my_electric_car ElectricCar()

test_start_engine(my_car)   Output: The engine starts with a roar.
test_start_engine(my_electric_car)   Output: The car starts silently with an electric motor.
```

This code demonstrates how polymorphism allows different objects to be processed by the same function or method, as long as they implement the required method. It also highlights how

Python's flexible type system supports polymorphic behavior through duck typing.

To further cement the understanding of object-oriented programming, it's valuable to discuss some practical considerations and best practices. When designing classes and objects, aim for encapsulation to safeguard the internal state and expose only necessary attributes and methods. Use inheritance judiciously to avoid creating overly complex hierarchies and ensure that the class relationships remain clear and maintainable.

Additionally, consider the principles of composition over inheritance. Composition involves building complex types by combining simpler ones, rather than extending existing classes. This approach can offer greater flexibility and avoid some of the pitfalls of deep inheritance chains. For instance, rather than creating a complex hierarchy of vehicle types, you might combine smaller components like engines and fuel systems into a vehicle class.

Lastly, always strive to make classes as modular and reusable as possible. By adhering to single responsibility and open-closed principles, you can create code that is easier to understand, test, and maintain. A class should focus on a single responsibility, and it should be open for extension but closed for modification, which promotes robustness and adaptability.

In summary, object-oriented programming in Python provides powerful tools for managing complexity and building scalable applications. Through classes, objects, inheritance, encapsulation, and polymorphism, developers can model real-world systems, enhance code reuse, and create more manageable and understandable codebases. By mastering these concepts, you will be well-equipped to tackle a wide range of programming challenges and develop sophisticated software solutions.

CHAPTER 9:

To structure packages effectively, it is crucial to understand the directory layout and the role of special files within a package. A package is typically organized as a directory containing multiple modules and a special `__init__.py` file. The presence of this `__init__.py` file distinguishes the directory as a package and allows it to be imported as a module. This file can be empty, but it can also execute initialization code for the package or set up the package's namespace.

Consider a package directory structure as follows:

```
mypackage/
  __init__.py
  module1.py
  module2.py
  subpackage/
    __init__.py
    module3.py
```

In this structure, `mypackage` is a package that contains two modules, `module1` and `module2`, as well as a subpackage named `subpackage`. The subpackage also has its own `__init__.py` file, which allows it to be imported independently.

To import modules from this package, you use dot notation to specify the path. For example, to import `module1` from `mypackage`, you would use:

```python
```

```
import mypackage.module1
```

To import a specific function or class from a module within the package, you can use:

```python
from mypackage.module1 import my_function
```

If you need to access a module within a subpackage, you extend the dot notation:

```python
import mypackage.subpackage.module3
```

Packages can also leverage relative imports to facilitate intra-package imports. For instance, if `module1` needs to import a function from `module2` within the same package, it can use:

```python
from .module2 import my_function
```

Relative imports are denoted by a leading dot, which refers to the current package level. Multiple dots can be used to move up the package hierarchy. For example, `from ..subpackage.module3 import another_function` refers to a module within a sibling subpackage of the current package.

The use of built-in modules and external libraries enhances the functionality provided by Python's standard library. Built-in modules are those that come with Python and do not require additional installation. These modules, such as `os`, `sys`, and `datetime`, cover a wide range of functionalities from interacting with the operating system to handling dates and times.

For instance, the `os` module provides functions to interact with the file system. You can use it to read or write files, navigate directories, and manage paths:

```python
import os

# Get the current working directory
current_dir = os.getcwd()
print(current_dir)

# List files in a directory
files = os.listdir(current_dir)
print(files)
```

External libraries, on the other hand, are third-party packages that extend Python's capabilities. These libraries are not included with Python and need to be installed separately, typically using package management tools such as `pip`. Examples include `numpy` for numerical computations, `requests` for HTTP requests, and `pandas` for data analysis.

To install an external library, you use the `pip` command. For instance, to install the `requests` library, you would run:

```
pip install requests
```

Once installed, you can import and use the library in your code just like any built-in module:

```python
import requests

response = requests.get('https://api.github.com')
print(response.status_code)
```

Managing dependencies and ensuring compatibility between

different packages is an essential part of using external libraries. Python environments and virtual environments, created with tools like `venv` or `virtualenv`, help manage dependencies by isolating packages required for specific projects. This isolation prevents version conflicts and ensures that each project has access to the necessary packages without interference.

When working with modules and packages, it is also important to adhere to best practices for code organization and documentation. Keeping modules and packages focused on specific functionalities makes code easier to understand and maintain. Writing clear docstrings and comments enhances the readability of the code, making it easier for others (and yourself) to understand the purpose and usage of each component.

In conclusion, understanding and effectively using modules and packages are crucial for writing modular, reusable, and maintainable Python code. By leveraging the capabilities of built-in modules, creating custom modules, and organizing them into packages, you can build complex systems with well-structured code. Incorporating external libraries and managing dependencies further extends Python's functionality, allowing you to tackle a wide range of tasks with efficiency and clarity.

Leveraging external libraries expands Python's capabilities significantly and enhances the functionality of your projects. These libraries are collections of pre-written code that address common programming tasks or provide specialized functions. External libraries are often maintained by the community or third-party organizations and can be easily integrated into your projects using package managers like `pip`.

To use an external library, you first need to install it. This is typically done via the command line with `pip`, Python's package installer. For example, to install the popular `requests` library, which simplifies making HTTP requests, you would run:

```bash
```

```
pip install requests
```

Once installed, you can import and use the library within your Python code just like any built-in module. For instance:

```python
import requests

response requests.get('https://api.example.com/data')
print(response.json())
```

In addition to installing external libraries, it's important to manage and document the libraries used in your project. This can be achieved using a `requirements.txt` file, which lists all the external dependencies your project needs. You can generate this file using:

```bash
pip freeze > requirements.txt
```

This command captures the exact versions of all installed packages. To later install these dependencies on a different machine or environment, you would use:

```bash
pip install -r requirements.txt
```

Maintaining a clean and organized structure for your projects is essential for readability and maintainability. Packages play a crucial role in this by grouping related modules into a single directory. For larger projects, a well-structured package layout can make it easier to navigate and understand the codebase. Proper naming conventions and clear documentation within your modules and packages further contribute to a well-maintained codebase.

It is also beneficial to be familiar with the concept of namespaces in Python, which helps prevent name conflicts. Each module and package in Python creates its own namespace, meaning that functions, classes, and variables defined in one module do not collide with those in another. This modular approach allows for cleaner code organization and avoids potential naming conflicts in larger projects.

In addition to managing code through packages, understanding how to work with modules and packages can significantly impact how you develop and maintain your software. For instance, when collaborating with others, adhering to a clear package structure and documenting your modules properly can facilitate easier code reviews and integration. Using external libraries can also accelerate development by providing tested solutions for common problems, allowing you to focus on more complex aspects of your application.

Finally, the exploration of Python's module system highlights the language's flexibility and robustness. By mastering modules and packages, you can harness Python's full potential to write modular, reusable, and maintainable code. This approach not only improves your own development practices but also enhances collaboration and code quality across projects.

CHAPTER 10:

To build upon the installation and basic usage of libraries such as NumPy and Pandas, it is essential to understand how these libraries interact with data. Pandas, in particular, excels in handling structured data through its `DataFrame` object, which supports operations such as filtering, grouping, and aggregating data. For instance, if we have a DataFrame named `df` with columns "A" and "B", filtering rows where column "A" is greater than 5 can be achieved with `df[df['A'] > 5]`. This syntax leverages boolean indexing, a powerful feature of Pandas for data manipulation.

Furthermore, Pandas provides comprehensive tools for data aggregation and summarization. For example, the `groupby` method allows for grouping data based on one or more columns and then applying aggregate functions. If we want to group data by column "A" and compute the mean of column "B" for each group, we can use `df.groupby('A')['B'].mean()`. This operation groups the data according to the unique values in column "A" and then calculates the mean of column "B" for each group, yielding a Series with the mean values.

In addition to these data manipulation techniques, Pandas offers robust functionality for reading from and writing to various file formats. The `read_csv` function is commonly used to load data from CSV files into a DataFrame, while `to_csv` allows exporting DataFrames to CSV format. For example, `pd.read_csv('data.csv')` reads data from a CSV file named 'data.csv' and returns it as a DataFrame. Conversely, `df.to_csv('output.csv')` writes the DataFrame `df` to a CSV file named 'output.csv'.

Beyond data manipulation and analysis, interacting with web APIs is another crucial aspect of extending Python's functionality. APIs, or Application Programming Interfaces, provide a way to access external services and data through predefined endpoints. The Requests library simplifies making HTTP requests to these APIs. To begin using Requests, one first needs to import the library with `import requests`.

A basic GET request to an API can be made using `requests.get(url)`, where `url` is the endpoint of the API. For instance, to fetch data from a public API that provides information on various countries, you might use `response requests.get('https://restcountries.com/v3.1/all')`. The `response` object contains the server's response, including the status code and the data. To access the data in JSON format, which is a common format for API responses, one would use `response.json()`. This method converts the JSON data into a Python dictionary or list, depending on the structure of the JSON.

In scenarios where APIs require authentication, the Requests library supports various methods to include credentials in the request. For APIs that use token-based authentication, the token is typically included in the request headers. For example, if you need to include an API key for authentication, you would add it to the headers using `headers {'Authorization': 'Bearer YOUR_API_KEY'}` and then pass this header to the `requests.get` method: `response requests.get(url, headersheaders)`.

Handling responses from APIs involves checking the status code to determine if the request was successful. A status code of 200 indicates success, while other codes might represent different types of errors or issues. For example, if `response.status_code 200`, you know that the request succeeded, and you can proceed to process the data. If the request fails, handling the error appropriately—such as retrying the request or logging the error—is important for robust application design.

Processing API responses often involves parsing and extracting relevant information. JSON data from APIs is usually nested, requiring careful navigation of the data structure. For instance, if the response JSON contains a list of dictionaries, each dictionary representing a country, you might extract the name of each country with a loop: `for country in response.json(): print(country['name'])`. This code snippet iterates through each dictionary in the list and prints the value associated with the 'name' key.

In addition to handling data, integrating external APIs into your Python applications may require additional considerations such as rate limits and error handling. Many APIs impose limits on the number of requests that can be made within a certain time frame to prevent abuse. It is important to review the API's documentation to understand these limits and implement appropriate handling mechanisms, such as exponential backoff strategies or request throttling.

By effectively leveraging libraries like NumPy and Pandas, along with mastering API interactions through Requests, you can significantly extend the capabilities of your Python applications. These tools provide a powerful means of data manipulation, analysis, and interaction with external services, enabling the development of more sophisticated and feature-rich applications.

When interacting with APIs, understanding the response structure is crucial for effective data extraction. After making a GET request, the response object returned by the `requests.get()` function includes several components, among which the `.json()` method is particularly useful for APIs that return data in JSON format. For instance, if an API response contains a JSON object, calling `response.json()` on the response object parses this JSON data into a Python dictionary or list, depending on the structure of the JSON. This conversion allows for straightforward manipulation and access to the data.

Handling API responses involves not just extracting data but also managing potential errors and exceptions. For example, a request might fail due to various reasons such as network issues or incorrect API endpoints. The `requests` library provides status codes in the response object that can be used to check for successful requests. The `response.status_code` attribute indicates the HTTP status code of the response. A status code of 200 signifies success, while codes like 404 or 500 denote errors. Implementing error handling is crucial for robust applications. For instance, checking if `response.status_code 200` before proceeding ensures that the data processing only occurs if the request was successful.

Authentication is another important aspect of working with APIs, especially for those that require user verification. Many APIs use API keys or tokens for authentication. These credentials are usually included in the request headers or as query parameters. For example, when an API requires an API key, it can be included in the headers as follows: `headers {'Authorization': 'Bearer YOUR_API_KEY'}`. The `requests.get(url, headersheaders)` function then sends this header along with the request. Properly managing and securing these keys is vital to prevent unauthorized access and to adhere to best practices in API usage.

In addition to GET requests, APIs often support other HTTP methods such as POST, PUT, and DELETE, which are used for creating, updating, and deleting resources, respectively. To use these methods with the Requests library, the `requests.post()`, `requests.put()`, and `requests.delete()` functions are employed. For instance, sending data to an API endpoint with a POST request involves specifying the data in the request body: `requests.post(url, data{'key': 'value'})`. This function sends the specified data to the server, where it can be processed according to the API's functionality.

Another critical aspect of API interaction is managing query parameters and payloads. Query parameters are appended to the URL to filter or modify the data returned by the API. They are included in the request by passing a dictionary to the `params` argument in `requests.get()`. For example, `requests.get(url, params{'param1': 'value1', 'param2': 'value2'})` sends a GET request with specified query parameters. On the other hand, payloads are used in POST and PUT requests to send data to the server. They can be included using the `data` or `json` arguments, depending on the content type expected by the API.

The integration of external resources into Python applications not only involves making requests but also parsing and using the retrieved data effectively. For instance, once the data is fetched from an API, it often needs to be transformed or cleaned before further use. Libraries such as Pandas can be instrumental in this process. Converting API response data into a DataFrame allows for powerful data manipulation techniques such as sorting, merging, and visualization. For example, if the API returns a list of records, converting this list into a DataFrame with `pd.DataFrame(api_data)` facilitates complex data operations and analysis.

Furthermore, understanding rate limits and usage policies of APIs is essential to ensure compliance and avoid disruptions in service. Many APIs impose limits on the number of requests that can be made within a certain time frame to prevent abuse. These limits are usually documented in the API's documentation and can affect how requests are scheduled or batched. Some APIs also provide headers in the response that indicate the remaining quota or the time until the rate limit resets. Monitoring and respecting these limits helps maintain a smooth and uninterrupted integration.

Overall, mastering the use of libraries and APIs significantly enhances the capabilities of Python applications. Libraries such as NumPy and Pandas expand Python's functionality to include sophisticated data analysis and manipulation, while APIs offer access to a vast array of external data and services. By understanding how to install and use these libraries, handle API requests and responses, manage authentication and errors, and process the retrieved data, one can build powerful and versatile Python applications that leverage both built-in and external resources effectively.

CHAPTER 11:

When working with Pandas, the ability to load data from various sources is a fundamental skill. Data can be imported from a variety of formats including CSV files, Excel spreadsheets, SQL databases, and JSON files. Each format has its own specific method within Pandas for reading data. For example, to load data from a CSV file, you can use the `pd.read_csv('filename.csv')` function. This method reads the CSV file and converts it into a DataFrame, automatically inferring column names and data types based on the file's content. Similarly, for Excel files, the `pd.read_excel('filename.xlsx')` function is used, which requires the `openpyxl` library if dealing with `.xlsx` files or `xlrd` for `.xls` files. This function can also be specified with parameters such as `sheet_name` to select a specific sheet from a workbook.

Once the data is loaded into a DataFrame, initial exploration and validation are necessary to understand its structure and content. Methods such as `df.head()` and `df.tail()` are invaluable for quickly viewing the first few and last few rows of the DataFrame, respectively. This initial inspection helps identify the basic structure of the dataset and whether the expected data is present. Additionally, `df.info()` provides a concise summary of the DataFrame, including the number of non-null entries, data types of each column, and memory usage, which can be useful for diagnosing issues related to data completeness and types.

The cleaning and transformation of data often involve several tasks. One common task is to correct data types. Data types in Pandas can be converted using the `astype()` method. For instance, if a column that should be numeric is mistakenly read as a string, you can convert it with `df['column_name'] df['column_name'].astype(float)`. Ensuring that data types are accurate is crucial for performing mathematical operations and analyses effectively.

Filtering and subsetting data are other common operations that enable more focused analysis. To select specific rows or columns, you can use various indexing techniques. For example, to select rows where a column value meets a certain condition, you might use boolean indexing: `df[df['column_name'] > value]`. This will return a DataFrame containing only the rows where the condition is met. Additionally, you can use the `loc[]` and `iloc[]` methods for more precise selection based on labels or integer positions, respectively. For instance, `df.loc[10:15, 'column_name']` retrieves values in the 'column_name' column from rows 10 through 15.

Handling categorical data and performing grouping operations are essential for summarizing and aggregating data. Pandas provides methods like `groupby()` to facilitate these tasks. For example, if you have a DataFrame with sales data, grouping by a categorical column such as "region" and then aggregating sales totals can be performed with `df.groupby('region')['sales'].sum()`. This operation groups the data by "region" and calculates the sum of sales for each region, producing a Series where the index represents regions and the values represent total sales.

Exploratory data analysis (EDA) involves generating descriptive statistics and visualizations to uncover patterns and insights within the data. Pandas offers a range of functions to compute descriptive statistics, such as `df.describe()`, which provides a summary of statistics including mean, standard deviation, and quartiles for numerical columns. This method is instrumental in quickly understanding the distribution and variability of the data. For visualizations, Pandas integrates with libraries like Matplotlib and Seaborn to create plots directly from DataFrames. Functions like `df.plot()` enable you to generate various types of plots, including line plots, histograms, and scatter plots, which can be customized further to reveal insights and trends within the data.

In summary, Pandas is a powerful tool for data analysis, providing robust mechanisms for data manipulation, cleaning, and exploration. By understanding how to create and manipulate DataFrames and Series, handle missing values, and perform basic analysis, you lay a solid foundation for more advanced data analysis tasks. Pandas' capabilities for data loading, cleaning, and exploratory analysis make it an indispensable library for anyone working with data in Python.

When exploring data with Pandas, one key aspect is performing exploratory data analysis (EDA), which helps to uncover patterns, detect anomalies, and test hypotheses. This process often involves generating summary statistics and visualizations to better understand the dataset. Pandas provides several methods for obtaining summary statistics through the `describe()` method, which generates descriptive statistics for numeric columns, including measures like mean, standard deviation, minimum, and maximum values. For categorical data, the `value_counts()` method is used to count the occurrences of each unique value in a column, providing insights into the distribution of categorical variables.

Data visualization is an integral part of EDA and can be achieved using libraries such as Matplotlib and Seaborn, which integrate seamlessly with Pandas. Although Pandas itself offers basic plotting functionality through its `plot()` method, more complex visualizations often require Matplotlib's `pyplot` interface or Seaborn's high-level functions. For example, to create a histogram of a numeric column, you can use `df['column_name'].hist()`, which generates a histogram displaying the frequency distribution of the data. For more sophisticated visualizations, like scatter plots or heatmaps, you would use Seaborn's functions such as `sns.scatterplot()` and `sns.heatmap()`, which offer greater customization and style options.

Handling missing values is a critical step in data cleaning and preparation. Missing values can arise from various sources, such as errors in data collection or incomplete records. Pandas provides several strategies for dealing with missing data. The `dropna()` method can be used to remove rows or columns that contain missing values, with the option to specify the threshold of non-null values required to retain a row or column. Alternatively, the `fillna()` method allows for filling missing values with a specified value, or using methods such as forward filling (`method'ffill'`) or backward filling (`method'bfill'`), where missing values are filled with the last or next available value in the column, respectively.

In addition to cleaning, transforming data is essential for effective analysis. Pandas supports various transformation operations, such as applying functions to columns or rows using the `apply()` method. This method can apply any function to each element in a column or row, allowing for complex transformations to be performed efficiently. For example, to compute the logarithm of values in a column, you can use `df['column_name'] df['column_name'].apply(np.log)`, assuming that NumPy has been imported as `np`. Grouping and aggregating data are also fundamental tasks that involve summarizing data based on certain criteria. The `groupby()` method allows for grouping data by one or more columns, and aggregate functions can be applied to each group. For example, `df.groupby('group_column').agg({'value_column': 'mean'})` computes the mean of the `value_column` for each group defined in `group_column`.

Exploratory data analysis often concludes with the development of insights and actionable recommendations. By combining statistical summaries, visualizations, and cleaned data, one can identify trends, outliers, and relationships that inform further analysis or decision-making. For instance, a time series analysis might reveal seasonal patterns or trends over time, which can be critical for forecasting and strategic planning.

The integration of Pandas with other libraries enhances its capabilities for data analysis. Libraries such as NumPy for numerical operations and Matplotlib or Seaborn for visualization complement Pandas, creating a comprehensive data analysis toolkit. Pandas' ability to handle and manipulate large datasets, combined with these additional libraries, enables sophisticated analyses that can drive valuable insights across various domains.

Mastering these foundational techniques in Pandas prepares one for more advanced data analysis tasks, such as time series analysis, machine learning preprocessing, and complex data transformations. Understanding and effectively utilizing Pandas' functionality is crucial for anyone engaged in data science or analytics, as it provides the building blocks for sophisticated data manipulation and analysis tasks.

CHAPTER 12:

When dealing with binary files, Python's file handling methods adapt to accommodate the unique requirements of binary data. To open a binary file, the mode 'b' must be appended to the file operation mode. For instance, using `open('image.jpg', 'rb')` opens the file in binary read mode, allowing the file's raw binary data to be accessed. Similarly, `open('output.bin', 'wb')` opens a file for binary writing, where data can be written in its raw binary format. The `read()` method, when used in binary mode, returns data as bytes, and the `write()` method writes bytes to the file. For example, `file.write(b'\x89PNG\r\n\x1a\n')` writes a sequence of bytes representing the start of a PNG file.

It is important to manage file resources carefully to prevent data corruption and resource leaks. Python provides a convenient way to handle files using the `with` statement, which ensures that files are properly closed after their suite finishes, even if an error occurs. For instance, `with open('example.txt', 'r') as file:` opens the file, and the file is automatically closed when the block inside the `with` statement is exited. This approach eliminates the need to explicitly call `file.close()`, thus reducing the risk of leaving files open inadvertently.

Error handling is another critical aspect of file operations. Files might not be accessible due to various issues such as incorrect file paths, lack of permissions, or hardware failures. Python's `try...except` block allows for the handling of these potential errors gracefully. For example, wrapping file operations in a `try` block and catching `IOError` exceptions enables you to manage file-related errors effectively. An example would be:

```python
try:
    with open('example.txt', 'r') as file:
        data file.read()
except IOError as e:
    print(f"An error occurred: {e}")
```

In this code snippet, if the file cannot be opened or read due to an `IOError`, the program prints an error message instead of crashing. This method of error handling is crucial for developing robust applications that can recover from or report file-related issues without failing abruptly.

Additionally, working with file paths requires an understanding of path handling to ensure cross-platform compatibility. Python's `os` module and `pathlib` library provide utilities for managing file paths. The `os.path` module includes functions like `os.path.join()` for constructing file paths in a platform-independent manner. For example, `os.path.join('folder', 'file.txt')` correctly constructs a file path regardless of the operating system. The `pathlib` library offers a more modern and object-oriented approach to path handling with classes such as `Path`. Using `Path('folder') / 'file.txt'` achieves the same result as `os.path.join()`, but with a more intuitive syntax.

File handling operations can be extended to more advanced use cases, such as reading and writing large files efficiently. For example, instead of reading an entire file into memory with `file.read()`, which may be impractical for very large files, you can read the file line by line using `file.readline()` or iterate over the file object itself. This approach allows for processing large files in a memory-efficient manner. Similarly, writing large amounts of data can be optimized by buffering data and writing it in chunks rather than all at once.

Overall, mastering file handling in Python involves understanding various file modes, handling different file types, managing file resources efficiently, and implementing error handling to deal with potential issues. Practical experience with these techniques will enable you to effectively create, modify, and manage files in a wide range of applications, from data processing to configuration management. As you apply these concepts in real-world scenarios, you will gain a deeper appreciation for the importance of proper file handling and its impact on the robustness and reliability of your applications.

When managing file paths in Python, it is essential to handle both absolute and relative paths accurately. An absolute path specifies the location of a file or directory from the root of the file system, providing a complete path string. For example, `/home/user/documents/file.txt` is an absolute path in Unix-like systems, while `C:\\Users\\user\\documents\\file.txt` is an absolute path in Windows. In contrast, a relative path specifies the location of a file relative to the current working directory of the script. For example, `data/file.txt` refers to a file located in a `data` subdirectory of the current working directory.

Python's `os` module facilitates path manipulations and provides functions such as `os.path.join()` to construct file paths in a platform-independent manner. This function combines directory names and file names into a single path, ensuring that the correct path separator is used for the operating system. For example, `os.path.join('data', 'file.txt')` produces `data/file.txt` on Unix-like systems and `data\\file.txt` on Windows. Additionally, `os.path.abspath()` returns the absolute path of a given relative path, and `os.path.exists()` checks if a specified path exists, which is useful for validating file paths before performing operations.

File handling also involves file permissions, which determine the accessibility of a file. Permissions are particularly relevant when reading from or writing to files, as insufficient permissions can lead to errors. In Unix-like systems, file permissions are managed using modes such as `r` (read), `w` (write), and `x` (execute). To handle permissions in Python, you might use the `os.chmod()` function to change file permissions programmatically. For instance, `os.chmod('example.txt', 0o644)` sets the permissions of `example.txt` to be readable and writable by the owner, and readable by others.

Another practical aspect of file handling is managing large files and optimizing performance. When dealing with large files, it is efficient to process the file in chunks rather than loading the entire content into memory. The `read(size)` method allows you to read a specific number of bytes at a time, which can be useful for handling large text or binary files. For example, reading a file in chunks of 1024 bytes can be achieved with:

```python
with open('largefile.txt', 'r') as file:
    while chunk : file.read(1024):
        process(chunk)  Replace 'process' with the actual processing function
```

In this code snippet, the file is read in 1024-byte chunks, and each chunk is processed individually. This approach reduces memory consumption and improves performance when handling large files.

Finally, ensuring that files are properly closed after operations is critical to avoid data corruption and resource leaks. The `close()` method is used to close a file explicitly, but the `with` statement provides a more robust solution. By using `with open('filename', 'mode') as file:`, Python ensures that the file is automatically closed when the block of code is exited, even if an exception occurs. This method eliminates the risk of forgetting to close the file and provides a cleaner and more maintainable approach to file management.

In summary, file handling in Python encompasses opening, reading, writing, and closing files, with specific modes and techniques tailored for different types of data. Understanding how to handle both text and binary files, manage file paths, handle permissions, process large files efficiently, and ensure proper resource management are essential skills for any Python developer. By mastering these concepts, you will be equipped to manage and manipulate files effectively in various real-world applications.

CHAPTER 13:

In addition to `try` and `except` blocks, Python provides the `else` block, which executes if no exceptions are raised in the `try` block. This is particularly useful for placing code that should run only when the `try` block succeeds without errors. For example, in a file handling scenario, you might want to read from a file only if it is successfully opened:

```python
try:
    file open('example.txt', 'r')
except FileNotFoundError:
    print("File not found.")
else:
    content file.read()
    print(content)
    file.close()
```

Here, the `else` block contains code that reads and prints the file content, but only if the file was opened successfully without any exceptions. If a `FileNotFoundError` occurs, the `except` block handles it, and the `else` block is skipped.

The `finally` block is another important component of exception handling. It executes regardless of whether an exception was raised or not. This block is typically used for clean-up actions that must be performed regardless of the outcome, such as closing files or releasing resources. For instance:

```python
try:
    file open('example.txt', 'r')
    content file.read()
    print(content)
except FileNotFoundError:
    print("File not found.")
finally:
    file.close()
```

In this example, the `finally` block ensures that the file is closed whether or not an exception occurs, preventing resource leaks.

Exception handling also involves creating custom exceptions to handle specific errors unique to your application. Custom exceptions are defined by subclassing the built-in `Exception` class and can be used to provide more informative error messages or handle specific conditions in a more controlled manner. For instance:

```python
class CustomError(Exception):
    pass

def check_value(value):
    if value < 0:
        raise CustomError("Value cannot be negative.")
    return value

try:
    result check_value(-1)
except CustomError as e:
    print(f"An error occurred: {e}")
```

Here, `CustomError` is a custom exception that is raised by the `check_value` function if the value is negative. The `except` block catches this specific exception and prints an error message.

When designing exception handling in your programs, it is crucial to follow best practices to enhance code readability and maintainability. Avoid using overly broad exception clauses such as `except Exception:` as they can inadvertently catch exceptions that were not anticipated or that should be handled differently. Instead, catch specific exceptions that you expect and can handle properly.

Furthermore, it's essential to avoid using exception handling for flow control. Exceptions should be reserved for handling genuine errors rather than regular control flow. This ensures that your error handling remains clear and that performance is not adversely affected by misuse of exceptions.

Properly documenting your custom exceptions and the scenarios in which they are raised also helps in maintaining code clarity and assisting other developers in understanding how to handle different error conditions appropriately.

In summary, exception handling in Python enables developers to write robust code that can manage errors gracefully. By using `try`, `except`, `else`, and `finally` blocks, you can control the flow of your program in the face of errors and ensure that resources are managed correctly. Custom exceptions allow for more precise error handling tailored to your application's needs, and following best practices helps maintain clean, efficient, and readable code.

When designing exception handling in Python, it is crucial to follow best practices to ensure that errors are managed efficiently and effectively. One such best practice is to catch specific exceptions rather than using a general `except` block. Catching specific exceptions allows you to handle different error types appropriately and avoid masking unexpected issues. For instance, catching a generic `Exception` can obscure the root cause of the problem, making debugging more challenging. Instead, you should catch specific exceptions and handle them according to their nature:

```python
try:
    Code that may raise multiple types of exceptions
    result some_operation()
except (FileNotFoundError, IOError) as e:
    print(f"An I/O error occurred: {e}")
except ValueError as e:
    print(f"Value error: {e}")
```

In this example, `FileNotFoundError` and `IOError` are handled together, while `ValueError` is managed separately. This approach provides clearer and more precise error handling.

Another important practice is to log exceptions for later analysis, especially in production environments. Logging allows you to track errors over time and gather information about their frequency and causes. The `logging` module in Python is a powerful tool for this purpose. You can configure logging to write error messages to a file or output them to the console. Here's an example of how to set up logging for exceptions:

```python
import logging

logging.basicConfig(filename'app.log', levellogging.ERROR)

try:
    Code that may raise an exception
    result perform_operation()
except Exception as e:
    logging.error(f"An error occurred: {e}", exc_infoTrue)
    print("An error occurred. Please check the log file.")
```

In this example, the `logging.error()` function records the exception details to a log file named `app.log`. The `exc_infoTrue` parameter includes traceback information in the log, which is valuable for diagnosing issues.

It is also important to avoid using exceptions for control flow. Exceptions should be reserved for handling genuine error conditions, not for regular control flow scenarios. Using exceptions to manage expected conditions can lead to less readable and less efficient code. For example, instead of using exceptions to handle cases where a file might not exist, you can check for the file's existence using `os.path.exists()`:

```python
import os

filename 'example.txt'

if os.path.exists(filename):
    with open(filename, 'r') as file:
        content file.read()
else:
    print("File does not exist.")
```

This approach avoids unnecessary exception handling and keeps the code more straightforward.

Furthermore, handling exceptions in functions that are part of larger applications requires careful consideration of how errors propagate. A well-designed function should handle its own exceptions where appropriate but also allow errors to propagate to higher levels if they cannot be resolved locally. This approach maintains the separation of concerns and allows the application to manage errors in a centralized manner. For example:

```python
def process_data(data):
```

```
try:
    Process data
    result perform_computation(data)
except ValueError as e:
    print(f"Data processing error: {e}")
    raise  Re-raise the exception to allow higher-level handling

def main():
    try:
        data get_data()
        process_data(data)
    except Exception as e:
        print(f"An unexpected error occurred: {e}")
```
``` 

In this scenario, `process_data` handles `ValueError` but re-raises it to allow the `main` function to handle it as well. This design ensures that errors are managed at the appropriate level of the application.

Lastly, effective exception handling also involves considering user experience. When an error occurs, it's important to provide meaningful feedback to the user, helping them understand what went wrong and, if possible, how to resolve it. Avoid exposing technical details that might confuse users; instead, present user-friendly messages that guide them through corrective actions.

By incorporating these practices into your Python programming, you enhance the robustness, maintainability, and user-friendliness of your applications. Exception handling is a powerful feature that, when used correctly, allows you to create programs that are resilient to errors and can handle unexpected conditions gracefully.
```

CHAPTER 14:

The `requests` module, for instance, simplifies making HTTP requests, allowing you to interact with web services and APIs with ease. To use `requests`, you first need to install it using `pip`:

```bash
pip install requests
```

Once installed, you can use it to send HTTP requests, such as fetching data from a web API:

```python
import requests

response requests.get('https://api.github.com')
print(response.json())
```

In this example, `requests.get()` sends a GET request to the GitHub API, and `response.json()` parses the JSON response. This demonstrates how third-party modules can greatly extend Python's capabilities.

Another crucial concept in Python programming is the organization of code into packages. A package is essentially a directory that contains multiple modules and a special `__init__.py` file. This file can be empty but serves to indicate that the directory should be treated as a package. Packages help you organize related modules into a directory hierarchy, making your codebase more manageable and modular.

For example, consider a project with a directory structure like this:

```
my_project/
    ├── my_package/
    │   ├── __init__.py
    │   ├── module1.py
    │   └── module2.py
    └── main.py
```

In this structure, `my_package` is a package containing two modules, `module1` and `module2`. The `__init__.py` file allows you to import modules from this package. Here's how you might structure the modules and import them:

module1.py:

```python
def function1():
    return "Function 1 from module 1"
```

module2.py:

```python
def function2():
    return "Function 2 from module 2"
```

main.py:

```python
from my_package import module1, module2

print(module1.function1())
print(module2.function2())
```

In this setup, `main.py` imports `module1` and `module2` from `my_package` and uses their functions. This approach enhances code organization and makes it easier to manage large codebases.

To further illustrate, suppose you need to create a package for mathematical operations. You could have a directory structure like:

```
math_operations/
    ├── __init__.py
    ├── arithmetic.py
    └── geometry.py
```

arithmetic.py:

```python
def add(x, y):
    return x + y

def subtract(x, y):
    return x - y
```

geometry.py:

```python
def area_circle(radius):
    import math
    return math.pi (radius 2)

def perimeter_circle(radius):
    import math
    return 2 math.pi radius
```

__init__.py:

```python
from .arithmetic import add, subtract
from .geometry import area_circle, perimeter_circle
```

In this example, `__init__.py` allows you to import all the functions from the `arithmetic` and `geometry` modules directly from the `math_operations` package:

```python
from math_operations import add, area_circle

print(add(5, 3))        Output: 8
print(area_circle(10))  Output: 314.1592653589793
```

This way, you can create a well-organized package that encapsulates related functionality, making your code more modular and easier to maintain.

Moreover, understanding the `sys.path` variable can be useful when dealing with modules and packages. `sys.path` is a list of directories that Python searches for modules when you use an `import` statement. By default, it includes the directory of the script being executed and standard library directories. You can modify `sys.path` to include additional directories where your custom modules or packages are located:

```python
import sys
sys.path.append('/path/to/your/modules')

import your_module
```

This feature is particularly helpful when you are working on larger projects with complex directory structures or when you need to include third-party modules that are not installed in the standard library paths.

By mastering modules and packages, you enhance your ability to write clean, organized, and reusable code. Effective use of these features contributes significantly to the overall quality and maintainability of your Python projects.

To create a package for mathematical operations, you might structure your project as follows:

```
math_operations/
    ├── __init__.py
    ├── algebra.py
    └── geometry.py
```

The `algebra.py` module might contain functions related to algebraic operations, while `geometry.py` might handle geometric calculations. The `__init__.py` file can be used to define what gets imported when the package is imported. Here's how you might set up these files:

algebra.py:

```python
def add(x, y):
    return x + y

def subtract(x, y):
    return x - y

def multiply(x, y):
    return x y

def divide(x, y):
    if y ! 0:
        return x / y
    else:
        raise ValueError("Cannot divide by zero")
```

geometry.py:

```python
import math

def area_of_circle(radius):
    return math.pi  radius  2

def perimeter_of_circle(radius):
    return 2  math.pi  radius
```

__init__.py:

```python
from .algebra import add, subtract
from .geometry import area_of_circle, perimeter_of_circle
```

In this setup, `__init__.py` allows you to control which functions are exposed when you import the `math_operations` package. By including `add`, `subtract`, `area_of_circle`, and `perimeter_of_circle`, users of your package can access these functions directly from the package level.

When using this package in another script, you can import the functions like so:

```python
from math_operations import add, area_of_circle

result  add(5, 3)
circle_area  area_of_circle(7)

print(result)  Output: 8
print(circle_area)  Output: 153.93804002589985
```

This approach encapsulates the functionality into well-defined modules and packages, promoting code reusability and organization. It also ensures that related functionalities are grouped together, making it easier to maintain and extend your code.

As your projects grow in complexity, it becomes even more important to manage your modules and packages effectively. Consider structuring your project to reflect the logical organization of your code. For instance, a larger project might include multiple sub-packages, each responsible for different aspects of the application. This hierarchical structure helps in maintaining a clear separation of concerns, facilitating easier debugging and development.

In addition to creating and using packages locally, you might want to share your packages with others or use packages developed by the community. Python's package index, PyPI, is the central repository where you can publish your own packages and download packages created by others. To publish a package to PyPI, you typically need to:

1. Create a `setup.py` file in your project's root directory. This file provides metadata about your package, such as its name, version, and dependencies:

```python
from setuptools import setup, find_packages

setup(
  name'math_operations',
  version'0.1',
  packagesfind_packages(),
  description'A package for basic mathematical operations',
  author'Your Name',
  author_email'your.email@example.com',
  url'https://github.com/yourusername/math_operations',
  install_requires[],
)
```

2. Build your package distribution:

```bash
python setup.py sdist bdist_wheel
```

3. Upload your package to PyPI using `twine`:

```bash
twine upload dist/
```

Once published, others can install your package using `pip`:

```bash
pip install math_operations
```

In summary, mastering modules and packages is essential for effective Python programming. Modules provide a way to organize code within a single file, while packages allow you to structure larger projects into directories. By following best practices for creating and managing modules and packages, you can enhance code readability, reusability, and maintainability. Whether you are building personal projects or contributing to open-source software, understanding these concepts will greatly improve your ability to write and manage complex Python applications.

CHAPTER 15:

Encapsulation is one of the fundamental principles of Object-Oriented Programming. It refers to the bundling of data (attributes) and methods (functions) that operate on that data into a single unit or class. This principle also involves restricting direct access to some of the object's components, which is often done to protect the integrity of the data. In Python, encapsulation is typically achieved through access modifiers.

While Python does not have strict access modifiers like some other languages, it provides a convention to indicate the visibility of attributes and methods. By prefixing an attribute or method with an underscore (`_`), you signal that it is intended to be protected and should not be accessed directly from outside the class. For example, consider a `BankAccount` class with a private balance attribute:

```python
class BankAccount:
    def __init__(self, owner, balance0):
        self.owner  owner
        self._balance  balance


    def deposit(self, amount):
        if amount > 0:
            self._balance + amount
            return f"Deposited {amount}. New balance is {self._balance}."
        else:
            return "Deposit amount must be positive."
```

```
    def withdraw(self, amount):
        if 0 < amount < self._balance:
            self._balance - amount
            return f"Withdrew {amount}. New balance is {self._balance}."
        else:
            return "Insufficient balance or invalid amount."

    def get_balance(self):
        return self._balance
```

In this class, `_balance` is marked as protected, indicating that it should not be accessed directly outside of the class. Instead, the methods `deposit`, `withdraw`, and `get_balance` are provided to manipulate and retrieve the balance, thus ensuring that the balance is not set to an invalid value and is kept consistent.

Inheritance is another key principle of OOP that allows one class to inherit attributes and methods from another class. This promotes code reuse and establishes a natural hierarchy between classes. When a class inherits from another, it is called a subclass or derived class, while the class being inherited from is referred to as the superclass or base class.

Consider a scenario where we have a base class `Animal` and a subclass `Dog` that extends `Animal`:

```python
class Animal:
    def __init__(self, name):
        self.name = name

    def speak(self):
```

```
        return f"{self.name} makes a sound."

class Dog(Animal):
    def speak(self):
        return f"{self.name} barks."

class Cat(Animal):
    def speak(self):
        return f"{self.name} meows."
```

In this example, `Dog` and `Cat` inherit from `Animal`. They both override the `speak` method to provide a specific implementation that reflects the sounds they make. This demonstrates polymorphism, where a method behaves differently based on the object that invokes it. By calling `speak` on an instance of `Dog` or `Cat`, we get different results despite using the same method name.

Polymorphism extends beyond method overriding. It also includes method overloading, though Python does not support method overloading in the traditional sense due to its dynamic nature. Instead, Python uses default arguments and variable-length argument lists to achieve similar functionality.

To further illustrate polymorphism, consider a scenario with a list of `Animal` objects:

```python
animals [Dog("Rex"), Cat("Whiskers")]

for animal in animals:
    print(animal.speak())
```

In this loop, the `speak` method is called on each `Animal` object. Due to polymorphism, the correct `speak` method for each object's type is executed, demonstrating how objects of different classes can be treated uniformly while still exhibiting behavior specific to their class.

Finally, to design effective and maintainable classes, it is important to follow best practices. Start by defining clear and coherent class responsibilities. Each class should have a single purpose and its methods should operate on its data to achieve this purpose. Avoid creating classes that try to handle too many responsibilities, as this leads to complex and hard-to-maintain code.

Utilize composition over inheritance when appropriate. While inheritance is a powerful feature, it can lead to tightly coupled code and difficulties in maintaining class hierarchies. Composition, where a class is built using instances of other classes, can often be a more flexible and maintainable approach.

In conclusion, Object-Oriented Programming provides a robust framework for designing and managing complex software systems. By understanding and applying the principles of encapsulation, inheritance, and polymorphism, you can create classes that not only model real-world entities effectively but also contribute to more organized, reusable, and maintainable code.

Polymorphism is another essential principle in Object-Oriented Programming that allows objects of different classes to be treated as objects of a common superclass. The key idea is that while different classes may have methods with the same name, they can exhibit different behaviors based on their specific implementations. This flexibility allows a single interface to be used with different underlying data types, making it easier to extend and maintain code.

To illustrate polymorphism, let's extend the previous example of the `Animal` class hierarchy. We can define a base class `Animal` with a method `make_sound`, and then create several subclasses that override this method to produce specific sounds:

```python
class Animal:
    def make_sound(self):
        raise NotImplementedError("Subclass must implement abstract method")

class Dog(Animal):
    def make_sound(self):
        return "Woof!"

class Cat(Animal):
    def make_sound(self):
        return "Meow!"

class Cow(Animal):
    def make_sound(self):
        return "Moo!"
```

In this example, `Animal` is the base class with a method `make_sound` that is intended to be overridden by subclasses. Each subclass (`Dog`, `Cat`, and `Cow`) provides its own implementation of `make_sound`. When you call `make_sound` on an object of one of these subclasses, the appropriate method is invoked, demonstrating polymorphism in action:

```python
animals [Dog(), Cat(), Cow()]

for animal in animals:
    print(animal.make_sound())
```

This code outputs:

```
Woof!
Meow!
```

Moo!
```

The `make_sound` method behaves differently depending on the actual class of the object, even though the method name is the same. This allows for a high level of abstraction and flexibility in your code.

In addition to polymorphism through method overriding, Python also supports polymorphism through method overloading, although it is less commonly used due to Python's dynamic nature. Method overloading allows a class to have multiple methods with the same name but different parameters. However, Python does not support traditional method overloading directly, as seen in statically-typed languages like Java or C++. Instead, you can achieve similar functionality using default arguments or variable-length argument lists:

```python
class Printer:
    def print_message(self, messages):
        for message in messages:
            print(message)

printer Printer()
printer.print_message("Hello, World!")
printer.print_message("Hello, World!", "Welcome to Python!")
```

In this example, the `print_message` method can accept any number of arguments, making it flexible to handle different use cases. This form of polymorphism enables the method to be used with varying numbers of inputs.

Another important aspect of OOP is the use of special methods, also known as dunder methods (short for double underscore), to control the behavior of objects in various situations. These methods include `__init__` for initialization, `__str__` for
```

string representation, and `__repr__` for a detailed string representation, among others. By overriding these methods, you can customize how objects are created, displayed, and interacted with.

For instance, consider modifying the `Car` class to include a custom string representation:

```python
class Car:
    def __init__(self, make, model, year):
        self.make make
        self.model model
        self.year year

    def __str__(self):
        return f"{self.year} {self.make} {self.model}"

    def __repr__(self):
        return f"Car(make'{self.make}', model'{self.model}', year{self.year})"
```

With these custom methods, when you print a `Car` object or view it in a debugger, you will see a more informative and readable output:

```python
my_car Car("Toyota", "Corolla", 2020)
print(my_car)  Output: 2020 Toyota Corolla
print(repr(my_car))  Output: Car(make'Toyota', model'Corolla', year2020)
```

These special methods enhance the usability and debugging experience when working with objects in Python.

In summary, Object-Oriented Programming in Python provides a robust framework for organizing code through classes and objects. By understanding and applying the principles of encapsulation, inheritance, and polymorphism, you can design software that is both modular and maintainable. Utilizing special methods further enhances the functionality and flexibility of your classes, allowing for a more intuitive and powerful programming experience.

CHAPTER 16:

In exploring inheritance further, it's crucial to understand method overriding, which allows a subclass to provide a specific implementation of a method that is already defined in its superclass. This capability enables subclasses to alter or extend the behavior inherited from the parent class.

Consider the `Vehicle` class example. Suppose we want to create a method in the `Car` class that provides a different implementation for starting the engine than the one provided by the `Vehicle` class. We can override the `start_engine` method in the `Car` class as follows:

```python
class Car(Vehicle):
    def __init__(self, make, model, num_doors):
        super().__init__(make, model)
        self.num_doors  num_doors

    def start_engine(self):
        return f"The {self.make} {self.model}'s engine roars to life with a turbo boost!"

    def open_trunk(self):
        return f"The trunk of the {self.make} {self.model} is now open."
```

Here, the `start_engine` method in the `Car` class provides a more specific description than the generic implementation in the `Vehicle` class. This customization is possible because `Car` inherits from `Vehicle` but can redefine inherited methods to fit its own requirements.

Polymorphism, another core principle of OOP, allows objects of different classes to be treated as objects of a common superclass. This is achieved through a common interface, typically through methods that are defined in a superclass but implemented differently in various subclasses.

To demonstrate polymorphism, consider that both `Car` and `Truck` classes implement a method named `start_engine`. Despite being different classes, both objects can use this method according to their specific implementations. Here's an example of how you might leverage polymorphism:

```python
def test_vehicle_start(vehicle):
  print(vehicle.start_engine())

Creating instances
my_car Car("Toyota", "Camry", 4)
my_truck Truck("Ford", "F-150", 1200)

Testing polymorphism
test_vehicle_start(my_car)     Outputs: The Toyota Camry's engine roars to life with a turbo boost!
test_vehicle_start(my_truck) Outputs: The Ford F-150's engine is starting.
```

In the `test_vehicle_start` function, the parameter `vehicle` can be of any class that implements the `start_engine` method. The actual method that gets executed is determined by the class of the object passed to the function, demonstrating how different implementations can be accessed through a common interface.

Additionally, Python supports multiple inheritance, where a class can inherit from more than one parent class. This allows a subclass to inherit attributes and methods from multiple sources, though it should be used judiciously to avoid complexity and ambiguity. Consider a scenario where we have a class `Electric` and another class `Luxury` that we want to combine:

```python
class Electric:
  def charge_battery(self):
    return "Charging the electric battery."

class Luxury:
  def provide_comfort(self):
    return "Providing luxury comfort features."

class ElectricLuxuryCar(Car, Electric, Luxury):
  def __init__(self, make, model, num_doors):
    super().__init__(make, model, num_doors)

    def show_features(self):
        return f"{self.start_engine()} {self.charge_battery()} {self.provide_comfort()}"
```

Here, `ElectricLuxuryCar` inherits from both `Car` and the `Electric` and `Luxury` classes. This demonstrates how multiple inheritance can be employed to create a more specialized class that integrates features from multiple sources.

Understanding and applying inheritance and polymorphism effectively allows developers to create more flexible and reusable code. These OOP principles not only help in organizing code logically but also facilitate easier maintenance and expansion. By defining clear relationships between classes and ensuring that methods can be overridden and utilized polymorphically, one can build systems that are both powerful and adaptable to changing requirements.

When designing classes with inheritance, it's important to also understand the concept of multiple inheritance. This feature allows a class to inherit attributes and methods from more than one parent class. Multiple inheritance can be powerful but also complex, as it introduces potential conflicts if the parent classes have overlapping attributes or methods. Python handles these situations using a method resolution order (MRO) which determines the order in which base classes are searched when executing a method.

For instance, consider the following example where a class `HybridCar` inherits from both `ElectricVehicle` and `GasolineVehicle`:

```python
class ElectricVehicle:
    def charge(self):
        return "Charging the electric vehicle."

class GasolineVehicle:
    def refuel(self):
        return "Refueling the gasoline vehicle."

class HybridCar(ElectricVehicle, GasolineVehicle):
    def start_engine(self):
        return "Starting the hybrid engine."

    def drive(self):
        return "Driving the hybrid car."
```

In this example, `HybridCar` inherits from both `ElectricVehicle` and `GasolineVehicle`. If there is no method conflict, the `HybridCar` class will have access to methods from both parent classes. However, if both parent classes define a method with the same name, the method resolution order will determine which implementation is used.

To see the MRO in action, you can use the `mro()` method of the class:

```python
print(HybridCar.mro())
```

This will output the method resolution order for the `HybridCar`, showing the sequence in which base classes are searched. Understanding the MRO is crucial when working with multiple inheritance to avoid unintended behaviors.

Another essential aspect of inheritance is the use of `super()` to call methods from the parent class. This function allows you to call a method from the parent class in a way that respects the MRO and provides flexibility in method overriding. Here's an example:

```python
class Base:
    def greet(self):
        return "Hello from Base."

class Derived(Base):
    def greet(self):
        base_greeting  super().greet()  Call the method from Base
        return f"{base_greeting} And hello from Derived."

Usage
obj  Derived()
print(obj.greet())
```

In this example, the `Derived` class overrides the `greet` method but still uses `super()` to call the `greet` method from the `Base` class. This approach ensures that the base class functionality is preserved while extending or modifying it in the derived class.

Polymorphism also plays a significant role in achieving flexible and maintainable code. By allowing different classes to be treated uniformly through a common interface, polymorphism facilitates the use of methods and attributes across various classes without needing to know the exact type of the object. This is particularly useful in situations where operations need to be performed on objects of different types that share a common set of behaviors.

Consider a scenario where you have different types of geometric shapes, such as circles and rectangles, each with its own implementation of a method to calculate the area. By defining a common interface for these shapes, you can write functions that operate on any shape without being concerned with the specifics of each shape's implementation:

```python
class Shape:
  def area(self):
      raise NotImplementedError("Subclass must implement abstract method.")

class Circle(Shape):
  def __init__(self, radius):
    self.radius radius

  def area(self):
    return 3.14159 (self.radius 2)

class Rectangle(Shape):
  def __init__(self, width, height):
    self.width width
    self.height height

  def area(self):
    return self.width self.height

def print_area(shape):
  print(f"The area is: {shape.area()}")

Usage
```

```
circle Circle(5)
rectangle Rectangle(4, 6)

print_area(circle)     Outputs: The area is: 78.53975
print_area(rectangle)  Outputs: The area is: 24
```
```

Here, the `Shape` class serves as an abstract base class with an abstract `area` method. Both `Circle` and `Rectangle` classes implement the `area` method according to their specific needs. The `print_area` function can operate on any object that adheres to the `Shape` interface, demonstrating how polymorphism allows for flexible and generic code that can work with different types of objects seamlessly.

In conclusion, inheritance and polymorphism are fundamental concepts in object-oriented programming that enhance code reuse and flexibility. By leveraging these principles, you can create a robust and extensible codebase, allowing for more effective modeling of real-world entities and behaviors.
```

CHAPTER 17:

Metaclasses offer profound customization for class creation and behavior, but decorators, while conceptually different, complement metaclasses by enhancing the functionality of functions and methods dynamically. Understanding decorators involves recognizing their role as a syntactic construct that allows you to modify or extend functions or methods without changing their actual code. They are particularly useful in scenarios where cross-cutting concerns, such as logging, access control, or modification, need to be applied consistently across different functions.

To grasp decorators, it is essential to comprehend their structure and usage. A decorator is essentially a function that takes another function as an argument and returns a new function that enhances or modifies the original one. This is accomplished using nested functions or closures. Here's a basic example to illustrate this concept:

```python
def my_decorator(func):
    def wrapper():
        print("Something is happening before the function is called.")
        func()
        print("Something is happening after the function is called.")
    return wrapper

@my_decorator
def say_hello():
    print("Hello!")
```

```
say_hello()
```

In this example, `my_decorator` is a decorator that wraps the `say_hello` function. When `say_hello` is called, the `wrapper` function inside `my_decorator` is executed first, adding additional behavior before and after the call to the original `say_hello` function. The `@my_decorator` syntax is a shorthand for applying the decorator, making the code cleaner and more readable.

Decorators can also accept arguments, allowing for more flexible configurations. For instance, you can create a decorator that logs the execution time of a function:

```python
import time

def time_it(func):
    def wrapper(args, kwargs):
        start_time time.time()
        result func(args, kwargs)
        end_time time.time()
        print(f"Function {func.__name__} took {end_time - start_time} seconds to execute")
        return result
    return wrapper

@time_it
def compute_sum(a, b):
    time.sleep(1)
    return a + b

compute_sum(5, 10)
```

In this example, the `time_it` decorator measures the time taken by the `compute_sum` function to execute. The `args` and `kwargs` syntax ensures that the decorator can handle functions with varying arguments. This demonstrates how decorators can be used to add functionality like logging and performance measurement in a reusable manner.

Another crucial aspect of decorators is their application to methods within classes. Method decorators allow you to enhance or modify class methods similarly to how you would with standalone functions. For example, consider a class that requires logging for its methods:

```python
def log_method_call(method):
    def wrapper(self, args, kwargs):
        print(f"Calling method {method.__name__} with arguments {args} and keyword arguments {kwargs}")
        result method(self, args, kwargs)
        print(f"Method {method.__name__} returned {result}")
        return result
    return wrapper

class Calculator:
    @log_method_call
    def add(self, x, y):
        return x + y

calc Calculator()
calc.add(5, 3)
```

In this example, the `log_method_call` decorator is applied to the `add` method of the `Calculator` class. The decorator logs information about the method call, including arguments and the result. This approach enables you to inject additional behavior into class methods without modifying their core logic.

Moreover, decorators can be stacked to apply multiple enhancements to a function. When multiple decorators are used, they are applied in the order from the innermost to the outermost:

```python
@time_it
@my_decorator
def say_hello():
    print("Hello!")
```

In this case, `my_decorator` is applied first, and then `time_it` is applied to the result of `my_decorator`. This stacking allows for flexible and layered modifications of functions.

In summary, metaclasses and decorators are powerful tools in Python that offer advanced customization capabilities. Metaclasses provide a means to control and modify class creation and behavior, allowing for sophisticated patterns and constraints. Decorators, on the other hand, offer a dynamic way to enhance or modify functions and methods, facilitating cross-cutting concerns and reusable code enhancements. Mastery of these concepts empowers you to write more flexible, maintainable, and robust Python code.

In addition to their practical applications, metaclasses and decorators also provide a window into the more intricate aspects of Python's object-oriented capabilities. Both mechanisms offer a high degree of control and flexibility, but they operate in distinct contexts and are used for different purposes.

Metaclasses, as previously discussed, are specialized classes whose instances are classes themselves. They are powerful tools that allow you to influence or control the creation and behavior of classes. By defining a metaclass, you can customize how classes are constructed and how their methods and attributes are set up. This can be particularly useful when you need to enforce certain patterns or rules across multiple classes.

For instance, consider a scenario where you want all classes in your codebase to automatically register themselves in a central registry. You could use a metaclass to achieve this. Here's a basic example of a metaclass that performs such registration:

```python
class RegistryMeta(type):
    registry {}

    def __new__(cls, name, bases, dct):
        cls_instance super().__new__(cls, name, bases, dct)
        RegistryMeta.registry[name] cls_instance
        return cls_instance

class BaseClass(metaclassRegistryMeta):
    pass

class MyClass(BaseClass):
    pass

print(RegistryMeta.registry)
```

In this example, `RegistryMeta` is a metaclass that maintains a class registry. Each time a new class is created that uses `RegistryMeta` as its metaclass, the class is automatically registered in the `registry` dictionary. This demonstrates how metaclasses can be employed to enforce patterns or conventions across a codebase.

Moving on to decorators, their flexibility extends beyond simple logging or timing functionalities. They can also be used to manage access control, memoization, and even to create domain-specific languages. For example, decorators can be utilized to restrict access to functions based on user roles:

```python
def requires_role(required_role):
    def decorator(func):
```

```
def wrapper(user_role, args, kwargs):
    if user_role ! required_role:
        raise PermissionError("You do not have the required role")
    return func(user_role, args, kwargs)
  return wrapper
return decorator

@requires_role('admin')
def perform_admin_task(user_role):
  print("Admin task performed")

perform_admin_task('admin')   Works fine
perform_admin_task('user')   Raises PermissionError
```

In this example, the `requires_role` decorator checks if the user has the required role before allowing the function to execute. This showcases how decorators can encapsulate complex logic that is reusable across different functions or methods.

Furthermore, decorators can be used for more advanced scenarios, such as class decorators. A class decorator is applied to an entire class and can modify its behavior or enhance it in various ways. For instance, you could use a class decorator to add logging to every method call within a class:

```python
def log_methods(cls):
  for attr_name in dir(cls):
    attr getattr(cls, attr_name)
    if callable(attr):
      setattr(cls, attr_name, log_method(attr))
  return cls

def log_method(method):
  def wrapper(args, kwargs):
    print(f"Calling method {method.__name__} with args {args} and kwargs {kwargs}")
```

```
    result  method(args, kwargs)
    print(f"Method {method.__name__} returned {result}")
    return result
  return wrapper

@log_methods
class MyClass:
  def method_a(self, x):
    return x  2

  def method_b(self, y):
    return y + 3

obj  MyClass()
obj.method_a(10)
obj.method_b(5)
```

Here, the `log_methods` decorator iterates over all methods of `MyClass`, applying the `log_method` decorator to each one. This results in logging information about each method call, including arguments and return values.

Both metaclasses and decorators underscore Python's flexibility in handling complex design patterns and code reuse. By leveraging these advanced features, you can write more modular, maintainable, and expressive code. They enable you to encapsulate behavior, enforce design patterns, and add functionality in a clean and reusable manner.

Understanding these tools is essential for mastering advanced Python programming and for building robust systems that can adapt to evolving requirements and complexities.

CHAPTER 18:

To insert data into the `users` table, you use the `INSERT INTO` SQL command. The following example demonstrates how to add a new user to the table:

```python
Insert a new record into the users table
cursor.execute('''
INSERT INTO users (name, email) VALUES (?, ?)
''', ('John Doe', 'john.doe@example.com'))
```

In this command, placeholders `?` are used to safely pass values into the SQL statement, which helps prevent SQL injection attacks. The `execute()` method takes a tuple containing the values to be inserted.

After executing the `INSERT INTO` command, it's important to commit the transaction using `conn.commit()`. This step ensures that the changes are saved to the database:

```python
Commit the transaction
conn.commit()
```

To retrieve data from the database, you use the `SELECT` statement. For example, to fetch all records from the `users` table, you can execute the following query:

```python
Fetch all records from the users table
```

```
cursor.execute('SELECT FROM users')
rows cursor.fetchall()
```

The `fetchall()` method retrieves all rows of the query result as a list of tuples. Each tuple represents a row from the table. You can then iterate over this list to process or display the data:

```python
for row in rows:
    print(row)
```

You might also need to update existing records. This is accomplished using the `UPDATE` statement. For instance, to update a user's email address, you can use the following code:

```python
Update a user's email address
cursor.execute('''
UPDATE users SET email ? WHERE name ?
''', ('new.email@example.com', 'John Doe'))
conn.commit()
```

Here, we use placeholders for the new email and the user's name to identify which record to update. As with insertions, it's essential to commit the transaction after making changes.

Deleting records from a database is done with the `DELETE` statement. For example, to delete a user with a specific name, you can use:

```python
Delete a user by name
cursor.execute('DELETE FROM users WHERE name ?', ('John Doe',))
conn.commit()
```

The `DELETE` statement removes the specified record(s) from the table, and the changes must be committed to take effect.

To ensure your database operations are handled properly, especially in scenarios where multiple operations are involved, it's good practice to use error handling with transactions. Here's an example of how you might use a `try...except` block to manage errors and ensure that transactions are rolled back in case of an error:

```python
try:
    Perform database operations
    cursor.execute('INSERT INTO users (name, email) VALUES (?, ?)', ('Jane Doe', 'jane.doe@example.com'))
    conn.commit()
except sqlite3.Error as e:
    print(f"An error occurred: {e}")
    conn.rollback()   Rollback in case of error
finally:
    Close the connection
    conn.close()
```

In this example, any `sqlite3.Error` exceptions are caught and reported, and the transaction is rolled back if an error occurs. This prevents partial changes from being committed to the database.

In addition to executing raw SQL commands, Python offers Object-Relational Mapping (ORM) libraries, which abstract away much of the SQL code required for database interactions. ORMs provide a way to interact with the database using Python objects, making it easier to manage database schemas and operations through object-oriented techniques. One popular ORM library for Python is SQLAlchemy. It allows you to define database schemas using Python classes and provides methods for querying and manipulating data without writing raw SQL.

Using SQLAlchemy involves several steps, starting with defining the database schema in Python classes. For example:

```python
from sqlalchemy import create_engine, Column, Integer, String
from sqlalchemy.ext.declarative import declarative_base
from sqlalchemy.orm import sessionmaker

Define the base class for declarative class definitions
Base declarative_base()

Define the User class that maps to the users table
class User(Base):
    __tablename__ 'users'

    id Column(Integer, primary_keyTrue)
    name Column(String, nullableFalse)
    email Column(String, uniqueTrue, nullableFalse)

Create an engine and bind it to the Base class
engine create_engine('sqlite:///example.db')
Base.metadata.create_all(engine)

Create a session to interact with the database
Session sessionmaker(bindengine)
session Session()
```

Here, the `User` class maps to the `users` table, and we use SQLAlchemy's `create_engine` and `sessionmaker` to manage database connections and transactions. This ORM approach simplifies many aspects of database management by allowing you to work with Python objects rather than raw SQL queries.

In summary, working with databases in Python involves connecting to a database, executing SQL commands, and handling results. SQLite provides a straightforward approach to managing databases, and ORMs like SQLAlchemy offer a higher-level abstraction to simplify database interactions. Understanding both methods allows for flexible and powerful data management in your Python applications.

To manage more complex database interactions, leveraging Object-Relational Mapping (ORM) libraries can be extremely beneficial. ORMs act as intermediaries between your Python code and the database, allowing you to interact with the database using Python objects rather than raw SQL queries. This abstraction helps simplify database operations and improves code readability and maintainability.

One of the most popular ORM libraries in Python is SQLAlchemy. SQLAlchemy provides a high-level interface to work with databases and supports multiple database engines beyond SQLite, including MySQL, PostgreSQL, and Oracle. To use SQLAlchemy, you first need to install it via pip:

```bash
pip install sqlalchemy
```

Once installed, you can begin by defining your database schema in Python classes. SQLAlchemy uses these classes to create tables and manage data. Here's an example of how to define a `User` class and set up a SQLite database using SQLAlchemy:

```python
from sqlalchemy import create_engine, Column, Integer, String
from sqlalchemy.ext.declarative import declarative_base
from sqlalchemy.orm import sessionmaker
```

Define the SQLite database engine
engine create_engine('sqlite:///example.db')

Create a base class for declarative class definitions
Base declarative_base()

```
Define the User class
class User(Base):
    __tablename__ 'users'

    id Column(Integer, primary_keyTrue)
    name Column(String)
    email Column(String)
Create all tables in the database
Base.metadata.create_all(engine)
```

In this snippet, `create_engine()` initializes the database connection, and `Base` serves as the foundation for defining your database schema. The `User` class represents a table in the database, with columns for `id`, `name`, and `email`. The `create_all()` method is used to generate the necessary database tables.

To interact with the database, you need to create a `Session` object, which handles the transactions. Here's how you can insert, query, update, and delete records using SQLAlchemy:

```python
Create a session
Session sessionmaker(bindengine)
session Session()

Insert a new user
new_user User(name'Jane Doe', email'jane.doe@example.com')
session.add(new_user)
session.commit()

Query users
users session.query(User).all()
for user in users:
    print(user.name, user.email)
```

```
Update a user
user session.query(User).filter_by(name'Jane Doe').first()
user.email 'jane.new@example.com'
session.commit()

Delete a user
session.query(User).filter_by(name'Jane Doe').delete()
session.commit()
```

In this example, `session.add()` adds a new record, and `session.commit()` finalizes the transaction. To retrieve records, `session.query()` is used, which allows you to filter and process results. The `filter_by()` method helps in finding specific records, while `delete()` removes them. As always, `session.commit()` ensures that changes are saved.

Besides SQLAlchemy, another popular ORM is Django's ORM, which is tightly integrated with the Django web framework. Django's ORM provides a similar set of features for defining models and performing database operations. To use Django's ORM, you would need to set up a Django project and define your models within Django's model system.

In addition to ORMs, understanding raw SQL and SQL execution is still valuable. For instance, when performing complex queries or database operations not easily handled by ORMs, direct SQL execution can be necessary. Here's an example of executing raw SQL using SQLAlchemy:

```python
from sqlalchemy import text

Execute raw SQL
with engine.connect() as connection:
    result connection.execute(text('SELECT FROM users'))
    for row in result:
        print(row)
```

```

In this case, `text()` constructs a raw SQL query, and `execute()` runs it. This approach provides flexibility and power, particularly for complex or custom queries.

By integrating ORM techniques with an understanding of raw SQL, you can effectively manage database interactions and leverage the strengths of both methods. ORMs offer simplicity and abstraction, while raw SQL provides direct control over database operations. Mastering both approaches enables you to handle various data management scenarios efficiently, ensuring that your Python applications can interact with databases in a flexible and robust manner.
```

CHAPTER 19:

To further develop your Flask application, you need to understand routing and how to handle different HTTP methods. Flask's routing mechanism allows you to define how different URLs should be processed by associating them with specific functions. In addition to handling GET requests, which are used to retrieve data from the server, Flask can also handle POST requests, which are used to submit data to the server.

You can define routes for different HTTP methods by using additional decorators. For example, to handle POST requests, you would modify your route decorator as follows:

```python
@app.route('/submit', methods['POST'])
def submit():
   data request.form['data']
    Process the data
    return 'Data received'
```

In this snippet, the `@app.route('/submit', methods['POST'])` decorator specifies that the `submit` function should handle POST requests to the `/submit` URL. The `request.form` object is used to access form data sent in the POST request. The `request` object is provided by Flask and contains data related to the HTTP request.

For handling form submissions, you would typically include a form in your HTML template. Here's an example of a simple form in an HTML file:

```html
<form action"/submit" method"post">
  <label for"data">Enter Data:</label>
  <input type"text" id"data" name"data">
  <input type"submit" value"Submit">
</form>
```

When the form is submitted, the browser sends a POST request to the `/submit` URL with the form data, which Flask then processes in the `submit` function.

Flask also provides support for URL variables, which allow you to pass dynamic data through URLs. You can define URL parameters in your route by using angle brackets. For example:

```python
@app.route('/user/<username>')
def show_user_profile(username):
    return f'User {username}'
```

In this example, `<username>` is a URL parameter that is captured and passed to the `show_user_profile` function as an argument. When a user navigates to `/user/johndoe`, Flask calls the function with `username` set to `johndoe`, and the response is `User johndoe`.

For more complex data interactions, you can use Flask's built-in support for rendering templates with dynamic content. The Jinja2 template engine, which is integrated with Flask, allows you to embed Python-like expressions and control structures within your HTML templates. For instance, you can use control flow statements to display different content based on conditions:

```html
{% if user %}
```

```
  <h1>Hello, {{ user.username }}!</h1>
{% else %}
  <h1>Hello, Guest!</h1>
{% endif %}
```

In this example, `{{ user.username }}` is a placeholder for a variable passed from your Flask view function. The `{% if %}` block checks if the `user` variable exists and displays a personalized greeting if it does.

Furthermore, you may need to handle static files, such as CSS and JavaScript, in your web application. Flask serves static files from a folder named `static` by default. You can reference these files in your templates using the `url_for` function:

```html
<link rel="stylesheet" href"{{ url_for('static', filename'style.css') }}">
```

This `url_for` function generates a URL for the static file, ensuring that the correct path is used regardless of the application's deployment configuration.

To enable Flask to manage larger and more complex applications, you should consider organizing your project into blueprints. Blueprints allow you to group related routes and views, making your application modular and easier to maintain. Here's a basic example of how to use blueprints:

```python
from flask import Blueprint

mod Blueprint('mod', __name__)

@mod.route('/hello')
def hello():
    return 'Hello from the blueprint!'
```

In your main application file, you would register the blueprint with your Flask app:

```python
from flask import Flask
from mymodule import mod

app Flask(__name__)
app.register_blueprint(mod)
```

Using blueprints helps you compartmentalize different parts of your application, making it more scalable and organized.

As you build more sophisticated web applications, you might also incorporate object-relational mapping (ORM) libraries like SQLAlchemy. ORMs allow you to interact with your database using Python classes and objects rather than writing raw SQL queries. SQLAlchemy integrates seamlessly with Flask, enabling you to manage your database models and queries within your Flask application.

Here's a brief example of using SQLAlchemy with Flask:

```python
from flask_sqlalchemy import SQLAlchemy

app.config['SQLALCHEMY_DATABASE_URI']                'sqlite:///example.db'
db SQLAlchemy(app)

class User(db.Model):
    id db.Column(db.Integer, primary_keyTrue)
        username    db.Column(db.String(80), uniqueTrue, nullableFalse)

    def __repr__(self):
        return f'<User {self.username}>'
```

```
```

In this example, `SQLAlchemy` is initialized with the Flask application, and a `User` model is defined to represent a database table. This setup allows you to perform database operations using Python code, abstracting away the complexities of raw SQL.

Building upon the foundation of routing and handling requests, it's essential to understand how to integrate databases into your Flask application. While SQLite is a lightweight and commonly used database, more robust solutions like PostgreSQL or MySQL might be preferable for larger applications. Flask itself does not include built-in support for databases, so you will often use an extension like Flask-SQLAlchemy, which provides an Object-Relational Mapping (ORM) interface for database interactions.

To use Flask-SQLAlchemy, you first need to install the package:

```bash
pip install Flask-SQLAlchemy
```

Once installed, you can integrate it into your Flask application by configuring it with the necessary database URI. Here's how you might set up Flask-SQLAlchemy with an SQLite database:

```python
from flask import Flask
from flask_sqlalchemy import SQLAlchemy

app Flask(__name__)
app.config['SQLALCHEMY_DATABASE_URI']        'sqlite:///mydatabase.db'
db SQLAlchemy(app)
```

In this configuration, `'sqlite:///mydatabase.db'` specifies the path to the SQLite database file. For other databases, you would adjust the URI accordingly. The `SQLAlchemy` object, `db`, is initialized with the Flask application instance, providing a way to interact with the database.

With Flask-SQLAlchemy, you define your database models as Python classes. Each class represents a table in your database, and class attributes represent columns. Here's a basic example of a model:

```python
class User(db.Model):
    id db.Column(db.Integer, primary_keyTrue)
    username db.Column(db.String(80), uniqueTrue, nullableFalse)
    email db.Column(db.String(120), uniqueTrue, nullableFalse)
```

In this model, the `User` class defines a table with three columns: `id`, `username`, and `email`. The `id` column is the primary key, uniquely identifying each record. The `username` and `email` columns are required and must be unique.

To create the database tables based on your models, you use the following commands:

```python
with app.app_context():
    db.create_all()
```

This command initializes the database and creates tables based on the defined models. It is typically run from a Python script or the interactive shell.

Once your models are defined, you can perform database operations such as querying, adding, updating, and deleting records. For example, to add a new user:

```python
new_user = User(username='john_doe', email='john@example.com')
db.session.add(new_user)
db.session.commit()
```

In this snippet, a new `User` instance is created and added to the session. The `commit()` method saves the changes to the database. Similarly, querying the database is straightforward:

```python
user = User.query.filter_by(username='john_doe').first()
```

This line retrieves the first `User` record with the username `'john_doe'`. Flask-SQLAlchemy provides a range of querying capabilities, allowing you to filter, order, and paginate results efficiently.

Integrating user input with database operations often involves forms. In Flask, the `WTForms` extension simplifies form handling and validation. To use `WTForms`, install it first:

```bash
pip install Flask-WTF
```

You can then define forms using `WTForms`. Here's an example of a form for creating a new user:

```python
from flask_wtf import FlaskForm
from wtforms import StringField, SubmitField
from wtforms.validators import DataRequired, Email

class RegistrationForm(FlaskForm):
    username = StringField('Username', validators=[DataRequired()])
    email = StringField('Email', validators=[DataRequired(), Email()])
```

```
    submit SubmitField('Register')
```

In this form, `StringField` creates text input fields for `username` and `email`, with validation to ensure that the fields are not empty and that the email is valid.

To use this form in a view function, render it in a template:

```python
from flask import render_template, redirect, url_for

@app.route('/register', methods['GET', 'POST'])
def register():
    form RegistrationForm()
    if form.validate_on_submit():
        user User(usernameform.username.data, emailform.email.data)
        db.session.add(user)
        db.session.commit()
        return redirect(url_for('index'))
    return render_template('register.html', formform)
```

Here, the form is validated upon submission. If valid, a new `User` is created and saved to the database. The `register.html` template should include the form rendering code.

Finally, when building web applications with Flask, consider using templates to separate HTML from your application logic. Flask uses the Jinja2 template engine, which allows you to embed dynamic content in HTML files. Templates facilitate the generation of dynamic web pages and ensure that your application remains maintainable and scalable.

In summary, integrating databases into your Flask application involves configuring and using SQLAlchemy or another ORM, defining database models, and performing CRUD operations. Handling user input through forms and validating it with

`WTForms` ensures that your application interacts with the database effectively. Leveraging templates with Jinja2 further enhances your ability to create dynamic and maintainable web applications.

CHAPTER 20:

With the Django project and app created, the next fundamental step is to define models. Models in Django are Python classes that represent database tables. Each model class is a blueprint for a table, and the class attributes define the columns of the table. To illustrate, let's create a simple blog model.

First, in the `models.py` file of your app directory, you define your model class. For example, in a blog app, you might create a `Post` model to represent blog posts. Here's what the `models.py` file might look like:

```python
from django.db import models

class Post(models.Model):
    title models.CharField(max_length100)
    content models.TextField()
    published_date models.DateTimeField(auto_now_addTrue)

    def __str__(self):
        return self.title
```

In this model, `Post` is a subclass of `models.Model`. Each attribute corresponds to a field in the database table. The `CharField` is used for short text fields such as the title of a post, while `TextField` is suitable for longer text like the content of the post. The `DateTimeField` with `auto_now_addTrue` automatically sets the field to the current date and time when the post is created. The `__str__` method provides a string representation of the model instance, which is useful for debugging and admin interfaces.

After defining models, you need to generate and apply migrations. Migrations are Django's way of propagating changes made to your models into the database schema. To create migrations for your models, run:

```bash
python manage.py makemigrations
```

This command generates migration files, which are essentially instructions for modifying the database schema. To apply these migrations and create the corresponding tables in the database, run:

```bash
python manage.py migrate
```

Now that your models are set up and migrated, you can proceed to create views. Views in Django handle the logic for processing requests and returning responses. They are defined in the `views.py` file of your app directory. For instance, you can create a view to display a list of blog posts:

```python
from django.shortcuts import render
from .models import Post

def post_list(request):
    posts Post.objects.all()
    return render(request, 'blog/post_list.html', {'posts': posts})
```

Here, `post_list` is a view function that queries all `Post` objects from the database and renders them using the `post_list.html` template. The `render` function combines a template with a context dictionary, which is passed to the template as variables.

Templates in Django are HTML files that define the structure of your web pages. They are stored in the `templates` directory within your app. For the `post_list` view, you need a corresponding template named `post_list.html`:

```html
<!DOCTYPE html>
<html>
<head>
  <title>Blog Posts</title>
</head>
<body>
  <h1>Blog Posts</h1>
  <ul>
    {% for post in posts %}
      <li>{{ post.title }} - {{ post.published_date }}</li>
    {% endfor %}
  </ul>
</body>
</html>
```

In this template, the `{% for post in posts %}` loop iterates over the `posts` context variable and generates a list item for each post. The `{{ post.title }}` and `{{ post.published_date }}` expressions display the title and published date of each post.

To connect your views to URLs, you must define URL patterns. In the `urls.py` file of your app, you specify which view should handle specific URL patterns. For example:

```python
from django.urls import path
from . import views

urlpatterns [
```

```
    path('', views.post_list, name'post_list'),
]
```

This configuration maps the root URL of the blog app to the `post_list` view.

Finally, for user authentication, Django provides built-in views and forms for login, logout, and password management. You can integrate these functionalities into your application by including the authentication URLs in your project's `urls.py` file:

```python
from django.contrib import admin
from django.urls import path, include

urlpatterns [
    path('admin/', admin.site.urls),
    path('blog/', include('blog.urls')),
    path('accounts/', include('django.contrib.auth.urls')),
]
```

Here, `include('django.contrib.auth.urls')` adds URL patterns for authentication provided by Django, such as login and logout.

This setup provides a comprehensive foundation for building a Django-based web application. You have learned to create models, views, and templates, connect them with URLs, and integrate user authentication. With these tools, you can build robust and scalable web applications that leverage Django's powerful features.

To complete the development of your Django application, you must handle templates and user authentication. Templates in Django are used to dynamically generate HTML content. They allow you to separate the presentation layer from the business logic. Templates are defined in HTML files with embedded

Django Template Language (DTL) syntax.

Create a directory named `templates` within your app directory. Inside this directory, create an HTML file for your view, for instance, `post_list.html`. In this file, you can use DTL to loop through and display the blog posts:

```html
<!DOCTYPE html>
<html>
<head>
  <title>Blog Posts</title>
</head>
<body>
  <h1>Blog Posts</h1>
  <ul>
    {% for post in posts %}
      <li>{{ post.title }} - {{ post.published_date }}</li>
    {% endfor %}
  </ul>
</body>
</html>
```

The `{% for post in posts %}` loop iterates through each post object passed from the view and displays its title and publication date. The `{{ post.title }}` syntax outputs the title of each post. This separation of logic and presentation helps maintain clean and manageable code.

In your `views.py`, modify the `post_list` view to render this template:

```python
from django.shortcuts import render
from .models import Post

def post_list(request):
```

```
posts Post.objects.all()
return render(request, 'post_list.html', {'posts': posts})
```

Here, `render` is a shortcut function that combines the template with the context (a dictionary containing data to be passed to the template) and returns an HTTP response.

To connect your view to a URL, you need to define URL patterns. In the `urls.py` file within your app directory, you map URLs to views. Define a URL pattern for your `post_list` view:

```python
from django.urls import path
from . import views

urlpatterns [
    path('', views.post_list, name'post_list'),
]
```

This code snippet maps the root URL of the app to the `post_list` view. When users navigate to the base URL of your application, Django will invoke the `post_list` view and render the `post_list.html` template.

With the core functionality in place, you should now address user authentication. Django provides built-in authentication mechanisms for managing user accounts, including login, logout, and password management. To incorporate authentication, you first need to create user authentication views and templates.

Django's built-in authentication system includes several useful views and forms. For example, to add login functionality, you can use Django's built-in `LoginView` and `LogoutView`. Update your `urls.py` file to include these views:

```python
```

```
from django.contrib.auth import views as auth_views

urlpatterns [
    path('login/', auth_views.LoginView.as_view(), name'login'),
    path('logout/', auth_views.LogoutView.as_view(), name'logout'),
    path('', views.post_list, name'post_list'),
]
```

These paths use Django's built-in views for handling login and logout. You must create corresponding templates to render these views. For instance, create a `registration/login.html` template for the login view:

```html
<!DOCTYPE html>
<html>
<head>
  <title>Login</title>
</head>
<body>
  <h1>Login</h1>
  <form method"post">
    {% csrf_token %}
    {{ form.as_p }}
    <button type"submit">Login</button>
  </form>
</body>
</html>
```

The `{% csrf_token %}` template tag adds a CSRF token to the form for security, and `{{ form.as_p }}` renders the form fields as paragraph elements.

For a complete user experience, you might want to handle user registration and password management. Django's authentication system also provides views and forms for user registration, password reset, and password change. You can use these built-in tools to build a comprehensive authentication system for your application.

Finally, once your application is developed and tested locally, you need to deploy it to a production environment. This involves setting up a web server, configuring a production database, and ensuring that your application is secure and performant. Django's documentation provides guidance on deploying applications to various environments, including cloud platforms like Heroku and AWS.

In summary, Django provides a powerful framework for developing web applications with its clean design and built-in tools. By creating models, views, templates, and incorporating user authentication, you can build a robust web application tailored to your needs. As you become more familiar with Django, you will be able to leverage its full potential to create complex and scalable web solutions.

CHAPTER 21:

Working with a `DataFrame` involves more than just creating and viewing data. You will often need to transform the data to make it more suitable for analysis. Pandas offers a wide array of functions to manipulate and transform data, such as filtering, sorting, and grouping.

Filtering data is essential for focusing on specific subsets of your data. This can be done using Boolean indexing. For example, if you want to filter a DataFrame to include only rows where the `Age` is greater than 30, you would use:

```python
filtered_df df[df['Age'] > 30]
```

Here, `df['Age'] > 30` creates a Boolean Series that is `True` for rows where the condition is met and `False` otherwise. This Series is then used to index `df`, resulting in `filtered_df` that contains only the rows where `Age` is greater than 30.

Sorting data is another common operation. You can sort a DataFrame by one or more columns using the `sort_values()` method. For instance, to sort the DataFrame by `Age` in descending order, you would use:

```python
sorted_df df.sort_values(by'Age', ascendingFalse)
```

The `by` parameter specifies the column to sort by, and `ascendingFalse` indicates that the sorting should be in descending order. If you want to sort by multiple columns, you can pass a list of column names to the `by` parameter and specify whether each column should be sorted in ascending or descending order.

Grouping data is particularly useful when you need to perform aggregate calculations on subsets of your data. The `groupby()` method allows you to group data based on the values in one or more columns and then apply aggregation functions such as sum, mean, or count. For example, to find the average `Age` for each `City`, you would use:

```python
grouped_df df.groupby('City')['Age'].mean()
```

Here, `groupby('City')` creates groups based on the `City` column, and `['Age'].mean()` calculates the mean age for each city. The result is a Series with the cities as the index and the average age as the values.

Data transformation often involves dealing with missing values. Missing data can arise from various sources and can be handled in several ways depending on the context and requirements of your analysis. Pandas provides several methods for addressing missing data, such as filling in missing values or dropping rows or columns with missing data.

To fill in missing values, you can use the `fillna()` method. For instance, if you want to replace all missing values in a DataFrame with a specific value, you can use:

```python
df_filled df.fillna(value0)
```

This will replace all `NaN` values in `df` with 0. Alternatively, you can use forward filling or backward filling techniques, which propagate the next or previous value in the column, respectively:

```python
df_filled df.fillna(method'ffill')  Forward fill
df_filled df.fillna(method'bfill')  Backward fill
```

Dropping missing values is another approach. If you choose to drop rows with missing values, you can use the `dropna()` method:

```python
df_dropped df.dropna()
```

This will remove all rows with at least one `NaN` value. You can also drop columns with missing values by specifying the `axis` parameter:

```python
df_dropped_cols df.dropna(axis1)
```

In addition to cleaning and transforming data, performing statistical analysis is a crucial aspect of data analysis. Pandas integrates many statistical functions that allow for the computation of descriptive statistics, such as mean, median, variance, and standard deviation.

For instance, to compute the mean and standard deviation of a column, you would use:

```python
mean_age df['Age'].mean()
std_age df['Age'].std()
```

Similarly, to compute other descriptive statistics such as the median, minimum, and maximum values, you can use:

```python
median_age df['Age'].median()
min_age df['Age'].min()
max_age df['Age'].max()
```

These statistics provide insights into the distribution and spread of your data, which are essential for understanding and interpreting the results of your analysis.

Lastly, visualization is a powerful tool for exploring and presenting data. While Pandas itself offers some basic plotting functions through its integration with Matplotlib, more complex visualizations may require additional libraries such as Seaborn or Plotly. For instance, to create a simple histogram of the `Age` column, you can use:

```python
df['Age'].hist()
```

This will produce a histogram showing the distribution of ages in your DataFrame. For more advanced visualizations, you can use Seaborn to create attractive and informative statistical graphics.

By mastering these techniques, you can leverage the full capabilities of Pandas to handle, analyze, and visualize data effectively, enabling more insightful and actionable conclusions from your data analysis tasks.

Handling missing data is a crucial aspect of data cleaning. Pandas provides several methods for detecting and managing missing values, which is essential for maintaining the quality and reliability of your dataset. Missing values can arise in various forms, such as `NaN` (Not a Number), `None`, or empty strings, and they need to be addressed appropriately depending on the context.

To detect missing values, you can use the `isna()` or `isnull()` methods, which return a DataFrame of the same shape as the original, with `True` indicating missing values and `False` otherwise. For instance, to find missing values in a DataFrame, you could execute:

```python
missing_data df.isna()
```

To get a summary of missing values in each column, use the `sum()` method:

```python
missing_summary df.isna().sum()
```

This will provide the count of missing values per column, helping you identify which columns require attention.

Handling missing data can be approached in several ways. One common method is to fill in missing values using the `fillna()` method. You can replace missing values with a specific value, such as zero or the mean of the column. For example, to fill missing values in the `Age` column with the mean age, you would do:

```python
mean_age df['Age'].mean()
df['Age'] df['Age'].fillna(mean_age)
```

Alternatively, if the missing values should be filled based on adjacent values or some other logic, `fillna()` supports forward filling and backward filling. Forward filling replaces missing values with the last known value, and backward filling uses the next known value. You can use:

```python
```

```
df.fillna(method'ffill', inplaceTrue)
```

Another strategy is to drop rows or columns with missing values using the `dropna()` method. This method removes rows or columns with any missing values by default. To drop rows with missing values:

```python
df_cleaned df.dropna()
```

If you need to drop columns with missing values, use:

```python
df_cleaned df.dropna(axis1)
```

Choosing the right method depends on the nature of your data and the extent of missing values. Dropping data may lead to loss of valuable information, while imputation may introduce biases if not handled carefully.

In addition to managing missing data, data transformation involves modifying or deriving new features from existing data. For example, you might need to create new columns based on existing ones. Suppose you have a column for `birth_year` and you want to create a new column for `age`. You can calculate `age` by subtracting the `birth_year` from the current year:

```python
import datetime
current_year datetime.datetime.now().year
df['age'] current_year - df['birth_year']
```

Data normalization and scaling are also crucial when preparing data for analysis, especially when working with machine learning models. Normalization involves adjusting values to a common scale, which can be done using methods such as min-max scaling or standardization. For min-max scaling, where values are scaled to a range between 0 and 1, you can use:

```python
df['scaled_column'] = (df['column'] - df['column'].min()) / (df['column'].max() - df['column'].min())
```

Standardization transforms data to have a mean of 0 and a standard deviation of 1, which is useful when features have different units. It can be achieved using:

```python
df['standardized_column'] = (df['column'] - df['column'].mean()) / df['column'].std()
```

Handling categorical data is another critical aspect of data transformation. Many machine learning algorithms require numerical input, so categorical data often needs to be encoded into numeric format. Pandas provides several methods for encoding, including one-hot encoding and label encoding. One-hot encoding creates a new binary column for each category, which can be performed using:

```python
df_encoded = pd.get_dummies(df, columns=['categorical_column'])
```

Label encoding assigns each category a unique integer. Although it's simpler, it may introduce unintended ordinal relationships between categories. Use `LabelEncoder` from `sklearn.preprocessing` for this purpose.

```python
from sklearn.preprocessing import LabelEncoder
encoder = LabelEncoder()
```

df['encoded_column']
encoder.fit_transform(df['categorical_column'])
```

Finally, exploratory data analysis (EDA) is an important step to understand your data better. Pandas integrates well with visualization libraries like Matplotlib and Seaborn to help in this process. For instance, to visualize the distribution of a numerical column, you can use:

```python
import matplotlib.pyplot as plt
df['column'].hist()
plt.show()
```

These tools and techniques for data manipulation and analysis form the backbone of data-driven decision-making, allowing you to clean, transform, and extract meaningful insights from your data efficiently.
```

CHAPTER 22:

Data visualization serves as a pivotal component in the data analysis process, enabling the transformation of raw data into graphical representations that are both accessible and interpretable. This section focuses on Matplotlib and Seaborn, two prominent libraries in the Python ecosystem that facilitate the creation of visualizations. By understanding and mastering these tools, one can significantly enhance the clarity and impact of data presentations.

Matplotlib, a versatile and powerful library, forms the cornerstone of Python-based data visualization. Its design is grounded in the principles of providing a comprehensive array of plotting functions that can be customized to meet specific needs. The library's core component is the `pyplot` module, which offers a stateful interface for plotting. To begin using Matplotlib, one must first import the library using the standard convention:

```python
import matplotlib.pyplot as plt
```

Once imported, creating a basic plot is straightforward. For example, plotting a simple line graph involves calling the `plot()` function with the desired data points. The following code snippet demonstrates how to create a basic line plot:

```python
x [1, 2, 3, 4, 5]
y [2, 3, 5, 7, 11]
```

```
plt.plot(x, y)
plt.xlabel('X-axis Label')
plt.ylabel('Y-axis Label')
plt.title('Simple Line Plot')
plt.show()
```

In this example, `plt.plot(x, y)` generates a line plot where `x` represents the data for the x-axis and `y` for the y-axis. The `xlabel()`, `ylabel()`, and `title()` functions are used to add labels and a title to the plot. The `show()` function then renders the plot in a window. Customization options are abundant, allowing for modifications to line styles, markers, colors, and more. For instance, to change the line style and color, one can pass additional arguments to the `plot()` function:

```python
plt.plot(x, y, linestyle'--', color'r', marker'o')
```

This command results in a dashed red line with circular markers at each data point.

While Matplotlib is highly customizable, it does require explicit commands to achieve the desired effects. This is where Seaborn comes into play. Seaborn builds upon Matplotlib by providing a higher-level interface for drawing attractive and informative statistical graphics. It simplifies the creation of complex visualizations and integrates seamlessly with Pandas DataFrames.

To use Seaborn, one must first install and import it. The installation can be done via pip:

```bash
pip install seaborn
```

Once installed, it is imported as follows:

```python
import seaborn as sns
```

Seaborn's strength lies in its ability to handle categorical and statistical data effortlessly. For example, creating a scatter plot with regression lines can be achieved using the `lmplot()` function. Consider the following code snippet, which uses Seaborn to plot a dataset:

```python
import seaborn as sns
import pandas as pd

Sample data
data pd.DataFrame({
    'x': [1, 2, 3, 4, 5],
    'y': [2, 3, 5, 7, 11]
})

sns.lmplot(x'x', y'y', datadata)
```

In this example, `lmplot()` automatically fits a linear regression line to the scatter plot of the data, providing a clear visual indication of the relationship between the variables. Seaborn also supports various types of plots, including histograms, box plots, and violin plots, each tailored for specific types of data analysis.

A key feature of Seaborn is its ability to handle data directly from Pandas DataFrames. This integration facilitates more straightforward data manipulation and plotting. For instance, plotting a box plot to visualize the distribution of data across different categories can be achieved with the `boxplot()` function:

```python
```

```
sns.boxplot(x'category', y'value', datadataframe)
```

Here, `dataframe` is a Pandas DataFrame containing the columns `category` and `value`. Seaborn's `boxplot()` function generates a box plot, which is useful for identifying outliers and understanding the distribution of data.

Customization in Seaborn is also robust, though somewhat different from Matplotlib. Seaborn offers a set of themes that can be applied globally to adjust the appearance of plots. For example, to apply a dark background theme, one can use:

```python
sns.set_style('darkgrid')
```

This command modifies the aesthetic elements of the plots, including grid lines and background color, making them more visually appealing. Additionally, Seaborn provides functions for creating complex visualizations, such as pair plots and heatmaps, with minimal code.

The integration of Matplotlib and Seaborn allows for extensive customization and detailed analysis. While Seaborn simplifies the process of creating complex plots, Matplotlib's low-level control ensures that highly specific visualizations can be achieved when needed. For a comprehensive data visualization approach, it is often advantageous to use both libraries in tandem, leveraging their respective strengths.

To summarize, Matplotlib and Seaborn are invaluable tools for data visualization in Python. Matplotlib offers detailed control and customization of individual plot elements, while Seaborn simplifies the creation of complex statistical graphics. By mastering both libraries, one can effectively communicate data insights through clear and impactful visualizations.

Seaborn builds upon Matplotlib, offering a higher-level

interface that simplifies the creation of complex statistical graphics. Its design philosophy emphasizes ease of use and aesthetics, making it an ideal choice for producing polished and informative visualizations with minimal code. Seaborn's integration with Pandas DataFrames enhances its functionality, enabling it to seamlessly handle structured data.

To start using Seaborn, one must first import the library alongside Matplotlib:

```python
import seaborn as sns
import matplotlib.pyplot as plt
```

Seaborn's utility becomes apparent when visualizing data distributions and relationships. For instance, the `sns.histplot()` function creates histograms, which are essential for understanding the distribution of a single variable. Consider the following example where we visualize the distribution of a dataset:

```python
import seaborn as sns
import pandas as pd

data pd.DataFrame({
    'values': [1, 2, 2, 3, 3, 3, 4, 4, 4, 4, 5, 5, 5, 5, 5]
})
sns.histplot(data['values'], bins5, kdeTrue)
plt.title('Histogram with Kernel Density Estimate')
plt.show()
```

In this example, `sns.histplot()` is employed to plot a histogram of the values, with the parameter `bins` specifying the number of bins and `kdeTrue` adding a Kernel Density Estimate (KDE) to illustrate the data distribution more smoothly. The integration of KDE is a notable feature in Seaborn that enriches the visualization by providing a continuous estimate of the probability density function of the variable.

When exploring relationships between variables, Seaborn's `sns.scatterplot()` proves invaluable. This function generates scatter plots that are particularly useful for visualizing the correlation between two continuous variables. Consider the following code snippet:

```python
import numpy as np

Generate sample data
np.random.seed(0)
x np.random.randn(100)
y 2 x + np.random.randn(100)

data pd.DataFrame({'x': x, 'y': y})
sns.scatterplot(datadata, x'x', y'y')
plt.title('Scatter Plot of x vs y')
plt.show()
```

Here, `sns.scatterplot()` is used to create a scatter plot of the variables `x` and `y`. The visual representation allows one to quickly identify any correlation or pattern between the two variables. Seaborn also supports additional features like fitting regression lines directly into scatter plots, using the `sns.regplot()` function:

```python
sns.regplot(datadata, x'x', y'y')
plt.title('Scatter Plot with Regression Line')
plt.show()
```

The `sns.regplot()` function not only plots the scatter points but also fits and displays a linear regression line, which provides insights into the strength and direction of the relationship between `x` and `y`.

Further extending its capabilities, Seaborn facilitates the creation of categorical plots through functions such as `sns.boxplot()` and `sns.violinplot()`. These plots are instrumental in summarizing and comparing distributions across different categories. For example, a box plot can be generated as follows:

```python
data pd.DataFrame({
    'category': ['A', 'B', 'C'] 20,
    'value': np.random.randn(60)
})
sns.boxplot(datadata, x'category', y'value')
plt.title('Box Plot of Values by Category')
plt.show()
```

In this instance, `sns.boxplot()` displays the distribution of `value` across different `category` groups, highlighting the median, quartiles, and potential outliers. Similarly, a violin plot can be used to provide a more detailed view of the distribution, including the density estimate:

```python
sns.violinplot(datadata, x'category', y'value')
plt.title('Violin Plot of Values by Category')
plt.show()
```

Violin plots offer a richer view of the data distribution by combining features of box plots and density plots, giving a comprehensive picture of the distribution's shape and spread.

For more complex visualizations, Seaborn's `pairplot()` function is highly effective in exploring relationships between multiple variables simultaneously. This function creates a matrix of scatter plots, where each subplot represents the relationship between a pair of variables. For example:

```python
iris sns.load_dataset('iris')
sns.pairplot(iris, hue'species')
plt.title('Pair Plot of Iris Dataset')
plt.show()
```

In this example, `sns.pairplot()` generates a grid of scatter plots for the `iris` dataset, with different colors representing different species. This comprehensive visualization aids in understanding how variables interact and in identifying potential patterns or clusters within the data.

Lastly, both Matplotlib and Seaborn offer extensive customization options to tailor visualizations according to specific requirements. Matplotlib's `rcParams` allows for global settings adjustments, such as figure size and font styles, while Seaborn's themes and style options simplify aesthetic adjustments. By leveraging these libraries' features, one can create a wide range of visualizations, from simple plots to intricate, publication-quality graphics, thus enhancing the ability to convey insights effectively and persuasively.

Introduction to Machine Learning with scikit-learn

Machine Learning (ML) represents a dynamic and rapidly evolving domain within data science, wherein algorithms are employed to discern patterns, make predictions, and inform decisions based on data. Scikit-learn, a robust and versatile library for Python, serves as an essential tool for implementing machine learning models. This library provides a range of algorithms for classification, regression, clustering, and more, alongside tools for data preprocessing and model evaluation. This discussion aims to introduce the fundamental aspects of machine learning with scikit-learn, including the types of algorithms available, data preparation techniques, and the process of training and evaluating models.

At its core, machine learning involves creating models that learn from data and generalize insights to new, unseen data. The first step in any machine learning workflow is understanding and preparing the data. Scikit-learn provides extensive functionalities for this purpose, including the ability to split data into training and testing sets, handle missing values, and scale features.

To start using scikit-learn, one must first install the library if it is not already available. This can be done using pip:

```bash
pip install scikit-learn
```

Once installed, scikit-learn can be imported into a Python script or notebook:

```python
import numpy as np
import pandas as pd
from sklearn.model_selection import train_test_split
from sklearn.preprocessing import StandardScaler
```

In machine learning, data preparation is crucial for building effective models. A typical dataset is divided into features (inputs) and target labels (outputs). For instance, if predicting housing prices, features might include the number of bedrooms, square footage, and location, while the target label would be the price.

An essential step is splitting the data into training and testing subsets. The training set is used to train the model, while the testing set evaluates its performance on unseen data. Scikit-learn's `train_test_split()` function facilitates this process:

```python
data pd.read_csv('data.csv')
X data.drop('target', axis1)  Features
y data['target']  Target labels

X_train, X_test, y_train, y_test train_test_split(X, y, test_size0.3, random_state42)
```

In this example, `data.csv` represents a dataset where 'target' is the column to be predicted. The `train_test_split()` function divides the dataset, with 30% allocated to the test set and the remainder to the training set. The `random_state` parameter ensures reproducibility.

Feature scaling is another critical aspect of data preparation, particularly when using algorithms sensitive to the scale of input features. Standardization, achieved through `StandardScaler`, normalizes features to have a mean of zero and a standard deviation of one:

```python
scaler StandardScaler()
X_train_scaled scaler.fit_transform(X_train)
X_test_scaled scaler.transform(X_test)
```

The `fit_transform()` method scales the training data, while `transform()` applies the same scaling to the test data, ensuring consistency.

With the data prepared, the next step is to select and apply a machine learning algorithm. Scikit-learn provides an extensive array of algorithms for various tasks. For classification tasks, algorithms such as Logistic Regression, Decision Trees, and Support Vector Machines (SVMs) are commonly used. For regression tasks, Linear Regression, Ridge Regression, and Lasso

Regression are prevalent choices.

To illustrate, let's consider a classification problem using Logistic Regression. Logistic Regression is a simple yet effective algorithm for binary classification problems. Here's how one might implement it using scikit-learn:

```python
from sklearn.linear_model import LogisticRegression
from sklearn.metrics import accuracy_score

model LogisticRegression()
model.fit(X_train_scaled, y_train)
y_pred model.predict(X_test_scaled)

accuracy accuracy_score(y_test, y_pred)
print(f'Accuracy: {accuracy:.2f}')
```

In this code, `LogisticRegression()` initializes the model, `fit()` trains it using the scaled training data, and `predict()` makes predictions on the test data. `accuracy_score()` then evaluates the model's performance by comparing the predicted labels with the true labels.

Beyond classification and regression, scikit-learn also supports clustering, a type of unsupervised learning where the goal is to group data into clusters based on similarity. One popular clustering algorithm is K-Means, which partitions data into `k` clusters. Here's how to apply K-Means clustering with scikit-learn:

```python
from sklearn.cluster import KMeans

kmeans KMeans(n_clusters3, random_state42)
kmeans.fit(X_train_scaled)
clusters kmeans.predict(X_test_scaled)
```

In this example, `KMeans()` initializes the clustering model with three clusters. The `fit()` method trains the model on the scaled training data, and `predict()` assigns cluster labels to the test data.

Evaluating model performance is integral to understanding how well a model generalizes to new data. Scikit-learn provides various metrics for evaluation. For classification models, metrics such as accuracy, precision, recall, and the F1 score are often used. For regression models, one might use metrics like Mean Absolute Error (MAE), Mean Squared Error (MSE), and R-squared.

In conclusion, scikit-learn offers a comprehensive suite of tools for implementing machine learning models. From data preparation to model training and evaluation, scikit-learn facilitates each step of the machine learning workflow. By leveraging these tools, one can build, evaluate, and refine machine learning models to address various predictive and analytical tasks.

Once the data is divided into training and testing sets, the next step involves preprocessing the data to ensure that the model performs optimally. Feature scaling is a common preprocessing technique that standardizes the range of features, making it easier for machine learning algorithms to converge. Scikit-learn provides the `StandardScaler` class to standardize features by removing the mean and scaling to unit variance. This is particularly useful for algorithms that are sensitive to the scale of input features, such as Support Vector Machines (SVMs) and k-Nearest Neighbors (k-NN):

```python
scaler StandardScaler()
X_train_scaled scaler.fit_transform(X_train)
X_test_scaled scaler.transform(X_test)
```

In this code snippet, `fit_transform()` is applied to the training data to compute the scaling parameters and then transform it accordingly. The `transform()` method is used on the test data to apply the same scaling parameters, ensuring consistency between training and testing data.

With the data prepared and scaled, one can proceed to select and implement machine learning algorithms. Scikit-learn offers a variety of algorithms, each suited for different types of tasks. For instance, in classification tasks where the goal is to predict categorical outcomes, algorithms such as Logistic Regression, Decision Trees, and Random Forests are commonly used. On the other hand, for regression tasks where the goal is to predict continuous outcomes, algorithms like Linear Regression and Ridge Regression are appropriate.

To illustrate, let's consider implementing a Logistic Regression model for a binary classification problem. Logistic Regression is a fundamental algorithm used to estimate probabilities and classify data points into two categories. Here is how you can use scikit-learn to train and evaluate a Logistic Regression model:

```python
from sklearn.linear_model import LogisticRegression
from sklearn.metrics import accuracy_score, confusion_matrix

model LogisticRegression()
model.fit(X_train_scaled, y_train)
y_pred model.predict(X_test_scaled)

accuracy accuracy_score(y_test, y_pred)
conf_matrix confusion_matrix(y_test, y_pred)

print(f'Accuracy: {accuracy:.2f}')
print('Confusion Matrix:')
print(conf_matrix)
```

In this example, `LogisticRegression()` initializes the model, and `fit()` trains it using the scaled training data. The `predict()` method generates predictions on the scaled test data, which are then evaluated using `accuracy_score()` to compute the model's accuracy and `confusion_matrix()` to provide a detailed breakdown of prediction results.

Beyond classification and regression, scikit-learn also supports clustering algorithms such as k-Means and hierarchical clustering. Clustering is an unsupervised learning technique used to group similar data points together. The k-Means algorithm, for example, partitions data into k clusters based on feature similarity:

```python
from sklearn.cluster import KMeans
import matplotlib.pyplot as plt

kmeans KMeans(n_clusters3, random_state42)
kmeans.fit(X_train_scaled)
clusters kmeans.predict(X_test_scaled)

plt.scatter(X_test_scaled[:, 0], X_test_scaled[:, 1], cclusters, cmap'viridis')
plt.title('k-Means Clustering')
plt.show()
```

Here, `KMeans()` is used to initialize the clustering algorithm with a specified number of clusters. After fitting the model on the scaled training data, predictions are made on the test data to assign cluster labels. A scatter plot visualizes the clustering results, where different colors represent different clusters.

Another important aspect of machine learning is model evaluation. Evaluating a model's performance involves assessing how well it generalizes to new data. Scikit-learn provides several metrics for evaluating models, including precision, recall, F1 score, and ROC curves. For classification tasks, metrics like precision and recall offer insights into how well the model performs on each class, while ROC curves and AUC scores provide a comprehensive evaluation of the model's discriminative power.

For regression tasks, common evaluation metrics include Mean Absolute Error (MAE), Mean Squared Error (MSE), and R-squared scores. These metrics help quantify the accuracy of predictions and the model's fit to the data:

```python
from sklearn.metrics import mean_squared_error, r2_score

y_pred_reg model.predict(X_test_scaled)
mse mean_squared_error(y_test, y_pred_reg)
r2 r2_score(y_test, y_pred_reg)

print(f'Mean Squared Error: {mse:.2f}')
print(f'R-squared Score: {r2:.2f}')
```

In this snippet, `mean_squared_error()` computes the average squared difference between predicted and actual values, while `r2_score()` assesses the proportion of variance explained by the model.

Overall, scikit-learn provides a comprehensive suite of tools for implementing and evaluating machine learning models. By mastering data preprocessing, algorithm selection, and model evaluation, one can harness the power of machine learning to extract valuable insights from data and drive informed decisions.

Once the model has been trained and evaluated, interpreting the results is crucial for understanding its performance and making improvements. The accuracy score provides a measure of how well the model's predictions match the actual outcomes, but it is often beneficial to explore additional metrics, especially in cases of imbalanced datasets or when different types of errors have varying costs.

The confusion matrix, which was computed earlier, is particularly useful for this purpose. It displays the number of true positives, true negatives, false positives, and false negatives, providing a more nuanced view of the model's performance. This breakdown helps in assessing not just overall accuracy but also the types of errors the model is making. For example, in a medical diagnosis scenario, false negatives might be more critical than false positives, making it important to evaluate the model's sensitivity and specificity.

For a more comprehensive evaluation, scikit-learn also provides other metrics such as precision, recall, and F1 score. These metrics can be computed using the following functions:

```python
from sklearn.metrics import precision_score, recall_score, f1_score

precision precision_score(y_test, y_pred)
recall recall_score(y_test, y_pred)
f1 f1_score(y_test, y_pred)

print(f'Precision: {precision:.2f}')
print(f'Recall: {recall:.2f}')
print(f'F1 Score: {f1:.2f}')
```

Precision measures the proportion of true positive predictions out of all positive predictions made by the model. Recall, on the other hand, measures the proportion of true positives out of all actual positive instances. The F1 score provides a harmonic mean of precision and recall, offering a balanced measure when dealing with imbalanced datasets.

Beyond these metrics, model tuning and improvement are essential aspects of machine learning. Hyperparameter tuning involves adjusting the parameters of a model to enhance its performance. Scikit-learn offers tools such as `GridSearchCV` and `RandomizedSearchCV` to automate this process. These methods systematically evaluate a range of hyperparameter values and select the best combination based on model performance.

For example, using `GridSearchCV` with a Logistic Regression model involves specifying a grid of parameters to test:

```python
from sklearn.model_selection import GridSearchCV

param_grid {
  'C': [0.1, 1, 10],
  'solver': ['liblinear', 'saga']
}

grid_search   GridSearchCV(LogisticRegression(), param_grid, cv5)
grid_search.fit(X_train_scaled, y_train)

print(f'Best Parameters: {grid_search.best_params_}')
```

In this case, `param_grid` defines the hyperparameters to be tested. The `GridSearchCV` function performs cross-validation to evaluate the performance of each parameter combination and identifies the optimal parameters.

Once the model has been tuned and optimized, it is crucial to validate its performance on new data. This step ensures that the model generalizes well beyond the training and testing sets used in the development phase. Cross-validation, a technique that involves partitioning the dataset into multiple subsets and training/testing the model on these subsets iteratively, is a robust method for assessing generalizability. Scikit-learn provides the `cross_val_score` function to facilitate this process:

```python
from sklearn.model_selection import cross_val_score

scores cross_val_score(LogisticRegression(C1, solver'liblinear'), X, y, cv5)
print(f'Cross-Validation Scores: {scores}')
print(f'Mean Cross-Validation Score: {scores.mean()}')
```

This function performs cross-validation with 5 folds, returning scores for each fold and the mean score, which provides an estimate of the model's performance across different subsets of the data.

In addition to supervised learning algorithms, scikit-learn also supports unsupervised learning techniques such as clustering and dimensionality reduction. For instance, the `KMeans` algorithm is used for clustering data into groups based on similarity. Dimensionality reduction techniques like Principal Component Analysis (PCA) can be employed to reduce the number of features while retaining the essential information.

Applying scikit-learn to machine learning tasks enables the construction of powerful predictive models. By mastering data preparation, model training, evaluation, and tuning, one can harness the capabilities of this library to tackle a wide array of real-world problems. Understanding these fundamental concepts lays the groundwork for exploring more advanced machine learning techniques and developing sophisticated models.

Networking Basics

Networking is a fundamental aspect of modern computing, enabling devices to communicate and exchange data across various types of networks. Understanding the basics of networking is crucial for developing networked applications and troubleshooting connectivity issues. This section introduces networking fundamentals using Python, focusing on socket programming, network protocols, and practical examples to build and manage networked applications.

At its core, socket programming forms the foundation of network communication. Sockets provide a mechanism for processes to communicate over a network by sending and receiving data. In Python, the `socket` library is the primary tool for working with sockets. This library supports both Transmission Control Protocol (TCP) and User Datagram Protocol (UDP), two fundamental protocols that handle data transmission in different ways.

To start, you need to understand the basic concepts of sockets and how they facilitate network communication. A socket is essentially an endpoint for sending or receiving data across a network. The two primary types of sockets are TCP sockets and UDP sockets. TCP sockets provide a reliable, connection-oriented communication channel, ensuring that data is transmitted accurately and in order. UDP sockets, in contrast, offer a connectionless communication method that does not guarantee delivery, order, or integrity of the data, but is often faster and more efficient for certain applications.

Creating a basic networked application involves setting up a server and a client. The server listens for incoming connections, while the client initiates the connection and communicates with the server. Let's explore how to implement a simple server and client using Python's `socket` library.

To create a basic server, you can use the following Python code:

```python
import socket

Create a TCP/IP socket
server_socket = socket.socket(socket.AF_INET, socket.SOCK_STREAM)
```

```
Bind the socket to an address and port
server_socket.bind(('localhost', 65432))

Listen for incoming connections
server_socket.listen()

print('Server is listening for connections...')

Accept a connection
client_socket, client_address  server_socket.accept()
print(f'Connected to {client_address}')

Receive data from the client
data  client_socket.recv(1024)
print(f'Received data: {data.decode()}')

Send a response to the client
client_socket.sendall(b'Hello, Client!')

Close the connection
client_socket.close()
server_socket.close()
```

In this example, `socket.socket(socket.AF_INET, socket.SOCK_STREAM)` creates a TCP/IP socket. The `bind()` method assigns the socket to a specific address and port, and `listen()` makes the server ready to accept incoming connections. The `accept()` method waits for a connection and returns a new socket object for communication with the client. The server receives data using `recv()` and sends a response using `sendall()`. Finally, both the client socket and server socket are closed to terminate the connection.

On the client side, you can use the following code to connect to the server and send data:

```python
import socket
```

```
# Create a TCP/IP socket
client_socket = socket.socket(socket.AF_INET, socket.SOCK_STREAM)

# Connect to the server
client_socket.connect(('localhost', 65432))

# Send data to the server
client_socket.sendall(b'Hello, Server!')

# Receive a response from the server
data = client_socket.recv(1024)
print(f'Received response: {data.decode()}')

# Close the connection
client_socket.close()
```

Here, `socket.socket(socket.AF_INET, socket.SOCK_STREAM)` creates the client socket, and `connect()` establishes a connection to the server. The client sends data with `sendall()` and receives a response using `recv()`. Finally, the client socket is closed to end the connection.

This basic setup demonstrates how to establish a simple communication channel between a server and a client. However, real-world applications often require more sophisticated handling of connections and data. For instance, you might need to handle multiple clients simultaneously, implement error handling, or manage more complex data structures.

To handle multiple clients, you would typically use threading or asynchronous I/O to manage concurrent connections. Python's `threading` library can be used to create a new thread for each client connection, allowing the server to handle multiple clients in parallel. Alternatively, Python's `asyncio` library provides an asynchronous framework for handling I/O operations without blocking, which is suitable for high-performance network applications.

In addition to socket programming, understanding network protocols is crucial for effective communication and troubleshooting. TCP and UDP are the most commonly used protocols, each suited for different types of applications. TCP ensures reliable and ordered delivery of data, making it ideal for applications that require accuracy, such as web browsers and email clients. UDP, on the other hand, is used for applications where speed is more critical than reliability, such as video streaming and online gaming.

In conclusion, networking fundamentals and socket programming provide a foundation for developing networked applications and understanding network communication. By mastering these basics, you can build and manage networked applications, troubleshoot connectivity issues, and leverage different network protocols to meet specific requirements.

To complement the server code, the client needs to establish a connection to the server and communicate by sending and receiving data. Here is a basic example of a client implemented in Python:

```python
import socket

Create a TCP/IP socket
client_socket = socket.socket(socket.AF_INET, socket.SOCK_STREAM)

Connect to the server
client_socket.connect(('localhost', 65432))

Send data to the server
client_socket.sendall(b'Hello, Server!')

Receive a response from the server
data client_socket.recv(1024)
```

print(f'Received data: {data.decode()}')

Close the connection
client_socket.close()
```

In this client code, `socket.socket()` creates a new socket object. The `connect()` method establishes a connection to the server at the specified address and port. The client sends a message using `sendall()`, which ensures that all data is transmitted. It then waits for a response from the server with `recv()`, which reads up to 1024 bytes of data. Finally, the `close()` method terminates the connection.

The server-client interaction in this example demonstrates the basics of a networked communication setup. It is crucial to understand how these components work together to facilitate data exchange between networked devices. The server listens for incoming connections, while the client initiates the connection and sends data to the server. After receiving a response, the client and server close their respective connections.

In addition to TCP, the `socket` library supports UDP sockets. UDP provides a simpler, connectionless alternative to TCP, which can be advantageous for applications where speed is more critical than reliability. Unlike TCP, UDP does not establish a connection before sending data and does not ensure that packets arrive in order or even that they arrive at all. This can make UDP more efficient for certain tasks but also less reliable.

To create a UDP server and client, the process is slightly different. Here is an example of a UDP server:

```python
import socket

Create a UDP socket
server_socket = socket.socket(socket.AF_INET,

```
socket.SOCK_DGRAM)

Bind the socket to an address and port
server_socket.bind(('localhost', 65432))

print('UDP server is listening for messages...')

Receive data from the client
data, client_address  server_socket.recvfrom(1024)
print(f'Received data from {client_address}: {data.decode()}')

Send a response to the client
server_socket.sendto(b'Hello, UDP Client!', client_address)

Close the socket
server_socket.close()
```

In the UDP server code, `socket.socket()` creates a UDP socket by specifying `socket.SOCK_DGRAM`. The `bind()` method associates the socket with a specific address and port. Unlike TCP, UDP sockets use `recvfrom()` to receive data, which also returns the address of the sending client. To respond, the server uses `sendto()`, specifying both the message and the client address. Finally, the socket is closed with `close()`.

Correspondingly, the UDP client can be implemented as follows:

```python
import socket

Create a UDP socket
client_socket        socket.socket(socket.AF_INET, socket.SOCK_DGRAM)

Send data to the server
client_socket.sendto(b'Hello, UDP Server!', ('localhost', 65432))

Receive a response from the server
data, server_address  client_socket.recvfrom(1024)
print(f'Received data from {server_address}: {data.decode()}')
```

```
Close the socket
client_socket.close()
```

In the UDP client code, `sendto()` sends data to the specified address and port, while `recvfrom()` receives a response from the server, including the server's address. After receiving the response, the client closes the socket.

Both TCP and UDP examples illustrate fundamental principles of socket programming. TCP ensures reliable, ordered delivery of data, making it suitable for applications where data integrity is crucial, such as web browsing or file transfers. UDP, on the other hand, is ideal for applications where speed is more critical than reliability, such as real-time video streaming or online gaming.

Understanding how to implement and use these protocols effectively is essential for developing robust networked applications. Additionally, it's important to be aware of common networking issues, such as latency, packet loss, and network congestion, which can impact application performance. Troubleshooting these issues often involves monitoring network traffic, analyzing log files, and employing diagnostic tools to identify and resolve problems.

In summary, mastering basic networking concepts and socket programming using Python provides a solid foundation for developing networked applications. By experimenting with TCP and UDP sockets, you gain practical experience in handling network communication and addressing various challenges that arise in networked environments.

In the UDP server example, the code snippet illustrates how to set up a UDP socket and handle incoming data:

```python
import socket
```

```python
# Create a UDP socket
server_socket = socket.socket(socket.AF_INET, socket.SOCK_DGRAM)

# Bind the socket to an address and port
server_socket.bind(('localhost', 65432))

print('UDP server is listening for messages...')

# Receive data from the client
data, client_address = server_socket.recvfrom(1024)
print(f'Received message: {data.decode()} from {client_address}')

# Send a response to the client
server_socket.sendto(b'Hello, Client!', client_address)

# Close the socket
server_socket.close()
```

In this UDP server code, the `socket.socket()` function creates a UDP socket with `socket.SOCK_DGRAM` specifying the use of UDP. After binding the socket to an address and port using `bind()`, the server listens for incoming messages with `recvfrom()`, which returns both the data and the address of the sender. This data is then printed, and a response is sent back to the client using `sendto()`, which specifies the address to send the response. Finally, the `close()` method terminates the socket.

Correspondingly, the UDP client implementation is straightforward:

```python
import socket

# Create a UDP socket
client_socket = socket.socket(socket.AF_INET,
```

```
socket.SOCK_DGRAM)

Send data to the server
client_socket.sendto(b'Hello, Server!', ('localhost', 65432))

Receive a response from the server
data, server_address client_socket.recvfrom(1024)
print(f'Received response: {data.decode()} from {server_address}')

Close the socket
client_socket.close()
```

The UDP client creates a socket similarly using `socket.SOCK_DGRAM`. It sends a message to the server using `sendto()`, specifying the destination address and port. The `recvfrom()` method is used to receive a response, capturing both the data and the server's address, which is then printed. As with the server, the `close()` method terminates the socket.

Understanding both TCP and UDP communication methods is essential for network programming. TCP is used when data integrity and order are critical, such as in web applications and file transfers, whereas UDP is suitable for applications requiring speed and efficiency over reliability, such as streaming and online gaming.

In practical network programming, handling errors and exceptions is crucial to ensuring robust and reliable applications. Network operations can fail due to various issues, including network congestion, incorrect addresses, or server unavailability. Scikit-learn's `socket` library provides mechanisms for handling such scenarios through exception handling.

Here's an example illustrating how to manage exceptions in a TCP server:

```python
import socket

try:
    # Create a TCP/IP socket
    server_socket = socket.socket(socket.AF_INET, socket.SOCK_STREAM)

    # Bind the socket to an address and port
    server_socket.bind(('localhost', 65432))

    # Listen for incoming connections
    server_socket.listen()

    print('Server is listening for connections...')

    # Accept a connection
    client_socket, client_address = server_socket.accept()
    print(f'Connected to {client_address}')

    # Receive data from the client
    data = client_socket.recv(1024)
    print(f'Received data: {data.decode()}')

    # Send a response to the client
    client_socket.sendall(b'Hello, Client!')

except socket.error as e:
    print(f'Socket error: {e}')

finally:
    # Ensure the sockets are closed
    client_socket.close()
    server_socket.close()
```

In this example, the `try` block encompasses the socket creation, binding, and communication processes. If any socket error occurs, the `except` block catches the exception and prints an error message. The `finally` block ensures that both the client and server sockets are closed properly, regardless of whether an error occurred.

Similarly, handling exceptions in UDP applications involves wrapping network operations in a `try` block and using appropriate exception handling mechanisms. Properly managing errors is crucial for developing reliable networked applications that can handle various network conditions and user scenarios.

In summary, mastering networking basics using Python's `socket` library equips developers with the tools necessary to build and manage networked applications effectively. Understanding TCP and UDP protocols, implementing basic server-client models, and handling exceptions are foundational skills in network programming. With these fundamentals, one can explore more advanced networking concepts and create robust applications that communicate over the internet or local networks.

Web Scraping

Web scraping is an invaluable technique for extracting data from websites, enabling users to gather information from various online sources efficiently. The process involves retrieving web pages and parsing their content to extract useful data, which can be used for research, analysis, or data aggregation. Python provides several libraries that facilitate web scraping, with BeautifulSoup and requests being among the most popular. This section will delve into the practical aspects of web scraping using these tools, outline best practices, and discuss the ethical considerations associated with scraping web data.

To begin with, the `requests` library is used to send HTTP requests to web servers and retrieve the content of web pages. It simplifies the process of making HTTP requests and handling responses, providing a straightforward interface for accessing web content. The following example demonstrates how to use `requests` to retrieve the HTML content of a web page:

```python
import requests

Send an HTTP GET request to the URL
response  requests.get('https://example.com')

Check if the request was successful
if response.status_code  200:
    Get the HTML content of the page
    html_content  response.text
else:
    print('Failed to retrieve the web page.')
```

In this code, `requests.get()` sends an HTTP GET request to the specified URL. The response object contains various attributes, including `status_code`, which indicates the success or failure of the request. If the status code is 200, indicating a successful request, `response.text` retrieves the HTML content of the page.

Once the HTML content is retrieved, the next step is to parse and extract data from it. BeautifulSoup, part of the `bs4` library, is a powerful tool for parsing HTML and XML documents. It provides methods for navigating and searching the parse tree, making it easy to locate and extract specific elements from the web page. To use BeautifulSoup, you first need to install it, which can be done using pip:

```bash
pip install beautifulsoup4
```

Here's an example of how to use BeautifulSoup to parse HTML and extract data:

```python
from bs4 import BeautifulSoup

Create a BeautifulSoup object with the HTML content
soup BeautifulSoup(html_content, 'html.parser')

Find the first <h1> tag in the HTML
h1_tag soup.find('h1')
if h1_tag:
    print('First <h1> tag:', h1_tag.text)
else:
    print('No <h1> tag found.')
```

In this example, `BeautifulSoup` is initialized with the HTML content and a parser type (`'html.parser'`). The `find()` method is used to locate the first occurrence of the `<h1>` tag in the document. If the tag is found, its text content is printed.

BeautifulSoup also allows for more complex queries. For instance, you can search for all instances of a particular tag or class, filter elements based on attributes, and navigate through the HTML tree structure. Consider the following example, where we extract all links from a page:

```python
Find all <a> tags in the HTML
links soup.find_all('a')

Extract and print the href attribute of each <a> tag
for link in links:
    href link.get('href')
    if href:
        print('Link:', href)
```

Here, `find_all()` retrieves all `<a>` tags, which are commonly used for hyperlinks. The `get()` method extracts the value of the `href` attribute, which specifies the URL of the link. This allows you to gather and process all links present on the page.

Web scraping involves not just retrieving and parsing data but also adhering to ethical guidelines and legal considerations. Many websites have terms of service or robots.txt files that specify scraping policies. It is essential to respect these guidelines to avoid legal issues and ensure fair use of website resources.

For example, some sites explicitly prohibit scraping or place limitations on how often and how much data can be scraped. Always check the `robots.txt` file of a site before scraping to understand its scraping policies. The `robots.txt` file is a standard used by websites to communicate with web crawlers and provide directives on which parts of the site can be crawled and scraped. It is accessible by appending `/robots.txt` to the site's base URL.

Furthermore, it is important to consider the impact of your scraping activities on the website's performance. Sending too many requests in a short period can place a heavy load on the server, potentially affecting the experience of other users. To mitigate this, implement polite scraping practices, such as rate limiting your requests, using exponential backoff strategies, and caching responses when possible.

By adhering to these best practices and ethical considerations, you can effectively and responsibly utilize web scraping techniques for a variety of applications while minimizing potential negative impacts on the websites you interact with.

With BeautifulSoup instantiated, we can now proceed to navigate and search through the HTML content. BeautifulSoup provides various methods to locate elements within the HTML structure. For instance, the `find()` method is used to find the first occurrence of a tag, while `find_all()` retrieves all occurrences of a tag. Here's an example of how to use these methods to extract data:

```python
Find the first <h1> tag in the HTML
h1_tag soup.find('h1')
print(h1_tag.text)

Find all <a> tags in the HTML
a_tags soup.find_all('a')
for tag in a_tags:
  print(tag.get('href'))
```

In this snippet, `find('h1')` searches for the first `<h1>` tag within the HTML content and prints its text. Similarly, `find_all('a')` retrieves all `<a>` tags, which are typically used for hyperlinks. The `get('href')` method extracts the value of the `href` attribute from each `<a>` tag, revealing the URLs linked by the page.

BeautifulSoup supports various methods for filtering and extracting data, such as selecting elements by class or id using CSS selectors. For instance, the `select()` method allows you to retrieve elements that match a CSS selector:

```python
Find elements with a specific class
elements soup.select('.class-name')
for element in elements:
  print(element.text)
```

Here, `select('.class-name')` retrieves all elements with the class `class-name`, and `element.text` extracts their textual content. CSS selectors provide a flexible way to navigate and extract specific parts of an HTML document.

In addition to BeautifulSoup and requests, it is essential to handle potential issues related to web scraping. These issues include dealing with dynamic content loaded via JavaScript, managing requests efficiently, and complying with website policies.

Dynamic content is often loaded asynchronously via JavaScript, which may not be present in the initial HTML retrieved by requests. To handle such cases, tools like Selenium or Scrapy can be employed. Selenium is a browser automation tool that can interact with web pages and retrieve dynamically loaded content. Scrapy, on the other hand, is a comprehensive web scraping framework that can handle more complex scraping tasks, including handling dynamic content.

Here is a brief example of using Selenium to retrieve dynamic content:

```python
from selenium import webdriver
from selenium.webdriver.chrome.service import Service
from selenium.webdriver.common.by import By
from selenium.webdriver.chrome.options import Options
```

Set up Selenium WebDriver
chrome_options Options()
chrome_options.add_argument("--headless")   Run in headless mode
driver   webdriver.Chrome(serviceService('/path/to/chromedriver'), optionschrome_options)

Navigate to the webpage
driver.get('https://example.com')

Retrieve dynamic content
element driver.find_element(By.ID, 'dynamic-content-id')
print(element.text)

Close the browser
driver.quit()
```
```

In this example, Selenium's WebDriver is configured to run in headless mode, which means it operates without opening a visible browser window. The `get()` method navigates to the specified URL, and `find_element(By.ID, 'dynamic-content-id')` retrieves an element with a specific ID that might be loaded dynamically. The `text` attribute extracts the content of the element, and `quit()` closes the browser.

Efficient management of requests is another critical aspect of web scraping. Sending too many requests in a short period can overwhelm the server and may lead to your IP address being blocked. To mitigate this, it is advisable to implement delays between requests and respect the website's `robots.txt` file, which specifies rules for web crawlers and scrapers.

Here's how to introduce delays between requests using Python:

```python
import time

Send a request to the server
response requests.get('https://example.com')

Introduce a delay between requests
time.sleep(1)  Delay for 1 second
```

The `time.sleep()` function pauses the execution for the specified duration, allowing you to space out requests and avoid overloading the server.

Finally, ethical considerations play a significant role in web scraping. It is crucial to respect the terms of service of websites and adhere to legal and ethical standards. Always check the website's `robots.txt` file to understand the rules for scraping and avoid scraping sensitive or personal information. Additionally, be mindful of the potential impact of your scraping activities on the website's performance and user experience.

By following these guidelines and best practices, you can ensure that your web scraping activities are conducted responsibly and effectively, leveraging the power of Python tools like BeautifulSoup and requests to gather valuable data from the web.

When dealing with dynamic content, where JavaScript alters the page after the initial load, `requests` and `BeautifulSoup` alone are insufficient. Selenium comes into play as it automates browser interactions, allowing you to retrieve the dynamically loaded data. Selenium simulates real user interactions by controlling a web browser through a script. Here's an example of how to use Selenium to scrape data from a page with JavaScript-loaded content:

```python
from selenium import webdriver
from selenium.webdriver.common.by import By
from selenium.webdriver.chrome.service import Service
from selenium.webdriver.chrome.options import Options
```

Set up Selenium options
chrome_options Options()
chrome_options.add_argument("--headless")   Run in headless mode (no browser window)

Path to your chromedriver executable
service Service('path/to/chromedriver')

Initialize the WebDriver
driver   webdriver.Chrome(serviceservice, optionschrome_options)

Open the web page
driver.get('https://example.com')

Wait for JavaScript to load the content

```
driver.implicitly_wait(10)   Wait up to 10 seconds for elements to appear

Extract data
elements   driver.find_elements(By.CSS_SELECTOR, '.dynamic-content')
for element in elements:
    print(element.text)

Close the WebDriver
driver.quit()
```

In this example, Selenium's `webdriver.Chrome()` is used to initiate a browser session. The `headless` mode allows the browser to run without displaying a graphical interface, which is useful for automated scripts. The `implicitly_wait()` method provides a way to wait for elements to load on the page, ensuring that the dynamic content is available before attempting to extract it. Finally, `find_elements(By.CSS_SELECTOR, '.dynamic-content')` retrieves all elements matching the specified CSS selector, and their text is printed out. The `quit()` method terminates the browser session once the task is complete.

Handling requests efficiently is also critical in web scraping to avoid overloading the server and to comply with website policies. When scraping multiple pages or making repeated requests, it's important to implement practices that minimize the impact on the target server. Implementing delays between requests using Python's `time.sleep()` function helps prevent excessive server load:

```python
import time

Delay between requests
time.sleep(1)   Sleep for 1 second
```

Additionally, using request headers such as `User-Agent` can help ensure that your requests are not mistakenly flagged as coming from a bot:

```python
headers {
    'User-Agent': 'Mozilla/5.0 (Windows NT 10.0; Win64; x64) AppleWebKit/537.36 (KHTML, like Gecko) Chrome/91.0.4472.124 Safari/537.36'
}

response requests.get('https://example.com', headersheaders)
```

Incorporating headers can make your requests appear as though they come from a standard web browser, which may help in avoiding detection and blocking.

Ethical considerations are paramount in web scraping. Always review and comply with the `robots.txt` file of a website, which specifies the pages that are allowed or disallowed for scraping. Ignoring these rules can lead to legal repercussions or being banned from accessing the site. It is also important to respect the terms of service of the website, as scraping might be prohibited or restricted.

Finally, consider the potential legal implications of scraping data, especially if the data is copyrighted or proprietary. Avoid scraping personal or sensitive information unless you have explicit permission to do so. Data privacy regulations, such as the General Data Protection Regulation (GDPR) in the European Union, impose strict rules on data collection and handling, which must be adhered to.

By following best practices and respecting legal and ethical guidelines, you can perform web scraping effectively while minimizing the risk of negative consequences. Understanding the tools and techniques available, from `requests` and

BeautifulSoup to Selenium, equips you to handle a variety of web scraping scenarios and build applications that can extract and utilize data from the web responsibly.

Working with APIs

Application Programming Interfaces (APIs) serve as a bridge between different software applications, enabling them to communicate and share data. APIs are pivotal in modern development, allowing developers to leverage external services and data sources without having to build everything from scratch. This section will cover how to make API requests using Python, handle JSON responses, and integrate data from various APIs into your applications. We will focus on RESTful APIs, which are widely used and follow the principles of Representational State Transfer (REST).

To begin with, interacting with an API typically involves sending an HTTP request to a specified URL and processing the response received from the server. Python's `requests` library is an excellent tool for making such HTTP requests. It provides a simple and intuitive API for interacting with web services. Below is an example of how to use `requests` to fetch data from a RESTful API:

```python
import requests

Define the API endpoint
url 'https://api.example.com/data'

Send an HTTP GET request to the API
response requests.get(url)

Check if the request was successful
if response.status_code 200:
    Parse the JSON data from the response
    data response.json()
    print(data)
```

```
else:
    print('Failed to retrieve data:', response.status_code)
```

In this code, `requests.get(url)` sends an HTTP GET request to the specified API endpoint. The `status_code` attribute of the response object is used to determine if the request was successful (HTTP status code 200). If successful, `response.json()` is used to parse the JSON data returned by the API. This data can then be used within your application as needed.

JSON (JavaScript Object Notation) is a common format for API responses due to its simplicity and readability. It represents data as key-value pairs and is easily parsed into Python dictionaries. Here's an example of a JSON response:

```json
{
  "name": "John Doe",
  "age": 30,
  "email": "john.doe@example.com"
}
```

In Python, this JSON data can be accessed like a dictionary:

```python
Assuming `data` is the parsed JSON response
name data['name']
age data['age']
email data['email']

print(f'Name: {name}')
print(f'Age: {age}')
print(f'Email: {email}')
```

Handling JSON data involves accessing the keys and values

directly, which is straightforward given that JSON is inherently similar to Python dictionaries.

When working with APIs, it's also essential to handle errors and exceptions gracefully. APIs may return various types of errors, such as invalid requests, unauthorized access, or server issues. Handling these errors properly ensures that your application can respond appropriately and maintain a good user experience. Here's how you might handle such situations:

```python
import requests

Define the API endpoint
url 'https://api.example.com/data'

try:
   Send an HTTP GET request to the API
   response requests.get(url)
     response.raise_for_status()    Raise an exception for HTTP errors

    Parse the JSON data from the response
   data response.json()
   print(data)
except requests.exceptions.HTTPError as http_err:
   print(f'HTTP error occurred: {http_err}')
except requests.exceptions.RequestException as req_err:
   print(f'Request error occurred: {req_err}')
```

In this snippet, `response.raise_for_status()` is used to raise an exception if the HTTP request resulted in an error status code. The `requests.exceptions.HTTPError` and `requests.exceptions.RequestException` classes are used to catch and handle specific errors that may occur during the request process.

APIs often require authentication, which can involve including an API key or token in your requests. This is typically done by adding an authorization header to your requests. Here's an example of how to include an API key in the headers of your request:

```python
import requests

Define the API endpoint
url 'https://api.example.com/data'

Define the API key
api_key 'your_api_key_here'

Set up the headers with the API key
headers {
    'Authorization': f'Bearer {api_key}'
}

Send an HTTP GET request with the headers
response requests.get(url, headersheaders)

Check if the request was successful
if response.status_code 200:
    Parse the JSON data from the response
    data response.json()
    print(data)
else:
    print('Failed to retrieve data:', response.status_code)
```

In this example, the `Authorization` header is used to pass the API key, which is often required for accessing protected resources. The `Bearer` prefix is a common convention for API token-based authentication.

Understanding how to work with APIs involves not only fetching and processing data but also adhering to best practices and ethical considerations. Always check the API documentation for usage limits, request quotas, and terms of service. Avoid making excessive requests that could overload the server, and respect the data privacy and usage policies outlined by the API provider.

When working with APIs, handling different types of HTTP requests beyond simple GET requests is essential. The `requests` library supports various methods, including POST, PUT, DELETE, and PATCH, each serving different purposes depending on the interaction with the API.

The POST method is often used to send data to an API to create or update resources. For example, to submit form data or upload information, you might use POST as follows:

```python
import requests

Define the API endpoint
url 'https://api.example.com/create'

Define the data to send in the request
payload {
    'name': 'John Doe',
    'email': 'john.doe@example.com'
}

Send an HTTP POST request to the API
response requests.post(url, jsonpayload)

Check if the request was successful
if response.status_code 201:
    print('Resource created successfully:', response.json())
else:
    print('Failed to create resource:', response.status_code)
```

In this example, `requests.post(url, jsonpayload)` sends a POST request with JSON data to the API. The `json` parameter in `requests.post()` automatically serializes the dictionary to JSON format. Upon success, indicated by a 201 status code, the response JSON is printed. POST requests are essential for operations that involve creating or modifying resources on a server.

PUT requests are used to update existing resources or create them if they do not exist. Here's how you might use a PUT request:

```python
import requests

Define the API endpoint
url 'https://api.example.com/update/123'

Define the updated data
payload {
  'name': 'Jane Doe',
  'email': 'jane.doe@example.com'
}

Send an HTTP PUT request to the API
response requests.put(url, jsonpayload)

Check if the request was successful
if response.status_code 200:
    print('Resource updated successfully:', response.json())
else:
    print('Failed to update resource:', response.status_code)
```

In this instance, `requests.put(url, jsonpayload)` sends an update request to the API, where `123` is the identifier of the resource being updated. PUT requests are suitable for scenarios where the entire resource is replaced with new data.

The DELETE method is used to remove resources from a server.

Here's an example of how to use DELETE:

```python
import requests

Define the API endpoint
url 'https://api.example.com/delete/123'

Send an HTTP DELETE request to the API
response requests.delete(url)

Check if the request was successful
if response.status_code 204:
    print('Resource deleted successfully')
else:
    print('Failed to delete resource:', response.status_code)
```

Here, `requests.delete(url)` sends a DELETE request to remove the resource identified by `123`. A successful deletion is indicated by a 204 status code, which means that the request was successful but there is no content to return.

The PATCH method is used for partial updates of resources, where only specific fields need to be modified. Here's an example of using PATCH:

```python
import requests

Define the API endpoint
url 'https://api.example.com/patch/123'

Define the partial data to update
payload {
    'email': 'new.email@example.com'
}

Send an HTTP PATCH request to the API
response requests.patch(url, jsonpayload)
```

```
Check if the request was successful
if response.status_code 200:
    print('Resource patched successfully:', response.json())
else:
    print('Failed to patch resource:', response.status_code)
```

In this example, `requests.patch(url, jsonpayload)` sends a PATCH request to update only the email field of the resource identified by `123`. PATCH is useful when you need to modify specific attributes without affecting the entire resource.

Additionally, APIs often require authentication and authorization to access protected resources. Common methods for API authentication include API keys, OAuth tokens, and Basic Authentication. For example, to use an API key, you might include it in the request headers:

```python
import requests

Define the API endpoint
url 'https://api.example.com/secure-data'

Define the API key
headers {
    'Authorization': 'Bearer YOUR_API_KEY'
}

Send an HTTP GET request with the API key
response  requests.get(url, headersheaders)

Check if the request was successful
if response.status_code 200:
    print('Data retrieved successfully:', response.json())
else:
    print('Failed to retrieve data:', response.status_code)
```

Here, the API key is included in the `Authorization` header, and `Bearer YOUR_API_KEY` is a common format for passing the token. The `headers` parameter in `requests.get()` includes these headers in the request.

Understanding these methods and their appropriate use cases will allow you to effectively interact with APIs, handle various types of requests, and integrate external data into your applications.

Handling errors and exceptions when working with APIs is crucial for building robust applications. The `requests` library provides mechanisms to handle HTTP errors and exceptions gracefully. The `requests` library raises exceptions for network-related errors, such as connection timeouts or invalid responses, which should be managed to prevent your application from crashing.

To handle potential exceptions during API requests, you can use a `try-except` block. Here is an example:

```python
import requests
from requests.exceptions import HTTPError, ConnectionError, Timeout, RequestException

url 'https://api.example.com/data'

try:
  response requests.get(url)
    response.raise_for_status()   Raise an HTTPError for bad responses (4xx and 5xx)
  data response.json()  Parse JSON response
  print(data)
except HTTPError as http_err:
  print(f'HTTP error occurred: {http_err}')
except ConnectionError as conn_err:
  print(f'Connection error occurred: {conn_err}')
```

```
except Timeout as timeout_err:
    print(f'Timeout error occurred: {timeout_err}')
except RequestException as req_err:
    print(f'Request error occurred: {req_err}')
```

In this code, `response.raise_for_status()` checks if the response status code indicates an error and raises an `HTTPError` if so. Specific exceptions such as `ConnectionError`, `Timeout`, and `RequestException` help handle different types of issues, ensuring that your application can react appropriately to various failure scenarios.

Additionally, integrating API data into applications often involves more than just fetching and displaying data. You may need to process the data, integrate it with other data sources, or store it in a database. To illustrate, consider an application that retrieves weather data from an API and stores it in a database. Here's how you might approach it:

```python
import requests
import sqlite3

Define the API endpoint
url 'https://api.weatherapi.com/v1/current.json'
params {'key': 'your_api_key', 'q': 'London'}

Fetch data from the API
response requests.get(url, paramsparams)
data response.json()

Connect to the SQLite database
conn sqlite3.connect('weather.db')
cursor conn.cursor()

Create a table if it doesn't exist
cursor.execute('''
CREATE TABLE IF NOT EXISTS weather (
```

```
    id INTEGER PRIMARY KEY AUTOINCREMENT,
    location TEXT,
    temperature REAL,
    condition TEXT
)
''')
```

Insert the API data into the database
location data['location']['name']
temperature data['current']['temp_c']
condition data['current']['condition']['text']

cursor.execute('''
INSERT INTO weather (location, temperature, condition)
VALUES (?, ?, ?)
''', (location, temperature, condition))

Commit the transaction and close the connection
conn.commit()
conn.close()
```
```

In this example, data from the weather API is fetched and parsed. Using `sqlite3`, the data is then stored in a SQLite database. The script first connects to the database and creates a table if it doesn't exist. The API data is then inserted into the table, and the connection is committed and closed.

In conclusion, working with APIs involves several key steps: making HTTP requests, handling different request types (GET, POST, PUT, DELETE), managing errors and exceptions, and integrating the data into applications. By understanding these aspects and leveraging libraries like `requests`, `BeautifulSoup`, and others, you can effectively interact with external services, retrieve and process data, and build powerful applications that leverage external data sources.

Database Interaction

Interacting with databases is a fundamental aspect of programming that allows developers to manage and manipulate data effectively. In Python, there are several libraries available for working with databases, including SQLite and SQLAlchemy. This section will introduce SQL concepts, demonstrate how to use these libraries for database interaction, and explore CRUD operations, schema design, and transactions.

Structured Query Language (SQL) is the standard language for managing relational databases. It enables you to perform various operations on data stored in relational databases, including querying, updating, inserting, and deleting records. SQL is essential for working with databases as it provides a uniform way to interact with different database systems.

SQLite is a lightweight, disk-based database engine that is included with Python's standard library through the `sqlite3` module. It is ideal for small to medium-sized applications and for development and testing purposes. Here's a brief overview of how to use SQLite with Python:

To start using SQLite, you first need to connect to a database. If the specified database file does not exist, SQLite will create it for you. The `sqlite3.connect()` function establishes a connection to the database. Once connected, you can create a cursor object, which allows you to execute SQL commands. The following example demonstrates creating a database, a table, and performing basic CRUD operations:

```python
import sqlite3
```

Connect to the database (or create it if it doesn't exist)
conn sqlite3.connect('example.db')

Create a cursor object
cursor conn.cursor()

```
Create a table
cursor.execute('''
  CREATE TABLE IF NOT EXISTS users (
    id INTEGER PRIMARY KEY AUTOINCREMENT,
    name TEXT NOT NULL,
    email TEXT UNIQUE NOT NULL
  )
''')
Insert a new record
cursor.execute('''
  INSERT INTO users (name, email)
  VALUES (?, ?)
''', ('John Doe', 'john.doe@example.com'))
Commit the transaction
conn.commit()
Query the database
cursor.execute('SELECT FROM users')
rows cursor.fetchall()
Print the results
for row in rows:
  print(row)
Close the connection
conn.close()
```
```

In this example, `sqlite3.connect('example.db')` connects to the `example.db` database file. The `CREATE TABLE` statement creates a table named `users` with columns for `id`, `name`, and `email`. The `INSERT INTO` statement adds a new record to the table. `conn.commit()` commits the transaction, making changes permanent. The `SELECT FROM users` query retrieves all records from the `users` table, and `cursor.fetchall()` fetches all rows from the result set. Finally, `conn.close()` closes
```

the database connection.

While SQLite is useful for smaller projects, SQLAlchemy is a more powerful and flexible library that provides an Object-Relational Mapping (ORM) system for Python. SQLAlchemy allows you to interact with databases using Python objects rather than raw SQL commands, making it easier to manage complex database interactions.

To use SQLAlchemy, you need to install it first:

```bash
pip install sqlalchemy
```

Here's an example of how to use SQLAlchemy to perform similar operations as shown with SQLite:

```python
from sqlalchemy import create_engine, Column, Integer, String
from sqlalchemy.ext.declarative import declarative_base
from sqlalchemy.orm import sessionmaker

Create an engine and a base class
engine create_engine('sqlite:///example.db')
Base declarative_base()

Define a User class to map to the users table
class User(Base):
    __tablename__ 'users'
    id Column(Integer, primary_keyTrue, autoincrementTrue)
    name Column(String, nullableFalse)
    email Column(String, uniqueTrue, nullableFalse)

Create the table
Base.metadata.create_all(engine)

Create a session
Session sessionmaker(bindengine)
session Session()
```

```
Add a new user
new_user User(name'John Doe', email'john.doe@example.com')
session.add(new_user)

Commit the transaction
session.commit()

Query the database
users session.query(User).all()

Print the results
for user in users:
    print(user.id, user.name, user.email)

Close the session
session.close()
```

In this SQLAlchemy example, `create_engine('sqlite:///example.db')` creates an engine that connects to the `example.db` SQLite database. `Base` is a declarative base class that maintains a catalog of classes and tables relative to that base. The `User` class maps to the `users` table, and `Base.metadata.create_all(engine)` creates the table in the database. The `sessionmaker` function creates a new session for database operations. After adding a new user and committing the transaction, `session.query(User).all()` retrieves all users from the `users` table.

Understanding how to design database schemas is another crucial aspect of database interaction. Schema design involves defining the structure of your database, including tables, columns, data types, and relationships between tables. Proper schema design ensures data integrity and optimizes query performance.

By mastering both SQLite and SQLAlchemy, you can handle a wide range of database interactions, from simple local databases to more complex relational databases.

When working with databases, understanding the concept of transactions is crucial. Transactions are sequences of operations performed as a single unit of work, ensuring that a series of database actions are completed successfully or none at all. This property, known as atomicity, is part of the ACID (Atomicity, Consistency, Isolation, Durability) properties of transactions that guarantee data integrity. Transactions help maintain a consistent state of the database even in the case of errors or unexpected failures.

In SQLite, transactions are managed using the `commit()` and `rollback()` methods. When a transaction is committed, all changes made during the transaction are saved to the database. If an error occurs, you can roll back the transaction to undo any changes made. Here's an example illustrating how transactions work in SQLite:

```python
import sqlite3

Connect to the database
conn sqlite3.connect('example.db')
cursor conn.cursor()

try:
   Begin a transaction
   cursor.execute('BEGIN TRANSACTION')

   Perform some operations
   cursor.execute('INSERT INTO users (name, email) VALUES (?, ?)', ('Alice Smith', 'alice.smith@example.com'))
   cursor.execute('INSERT INTO users (name, email) VALUES (?, ?)', ('Bob Johnson', 'bob.johnson@example.com'))

   Commit the transaction
   conn.commit()
   print('Transaction committed successfully.')
```

```
except Exception as e:
    Roll back the transaction in case of an error
    conn.rollback()
    print('Transaction rolled back due to an error:', e)

finally:
    Close the connection
    conn.close()
```

In this code, the transaction begins with `cursor.execute('BEGIN TRANSACTION')`. If any exception occurs during the operations, `conn.rollback()` undoes the changes. If no exceptions are raised, `conn.commit()` finalizes the changes.

Moving beyond SQLite, SQLAlchemy is a powerful and flexible ORM (Object-Relational Mapping) library for Python that provides a high-level abstraction for interacting with relational databases. SQLAlchemy allows you to work with databases using Python classes and objects, simplifying the management of database schemas and queries.

To use SQLAlchemy, you first need to install it using pip:

```sh
pip install sqlalchemy
```

With SQLAlchemy, you define database models as Python classes. These models represent tables in the database. SQLAlchemy automatically maps class attributes to table columns. Here's a basic example of defining a model and performing operations using SQLAlchemy:

```python
from sqlalchemy import create_engine, Column, Integer, String
from sqlalchemy.ext.declarative import declarative_base
from sqlalchemy.orm import sessionmaker
```

```
Define the SQLite database URL
DATABASE_URL 'sqlite:///example.db'

Create an engine and a base class
engine create_engine(DATABASE_URL, echoTrue)
Base declarative_base()

Define a User model
class User(Base):
    __tablename__ 'users'

    id Column(Integer, primary_keyTrue, autoincrementTrue)
    name Column(String, nullableFalse)
    email Column(String, uniqueTrue, nullableFalse)

Create the table
Base.metadata.create_all(engine)

Create a session
Session sessionmaker(bindengine)
session Session()

Add a new user
new_user User(name'Charlie Brown', email'charlie.brown@example.com')
session.add(new_user)
session.commit()

Query the database
users session.query(User).all()
for user in users:
    print(user.name, user.email)

Close the session
session.close()
```

In this example, `create_engine()` establishes a connection to the SQLite database. The `Base` class is used to define the `User` model, which represents the `users` table. `Base.metadata.create_all(engine)` creates the table in the database. The `Session` class is used to manage transactions and queries. Operations such as adding a new user and querying the database are simplified with SQLAlchemy's ORM capabilities.

SQLAlchemy also supports advanced features such as relationships between models, complex queries, and migrations. The flexibility and power of SQLAlchemy make it an excellent choice for applications that require more sophisticated database interactions.

In summary, effective database interaction involves understanding and applying concepts of SQL and transactions, utilizing libraries such as SQLite for lightweight database management, and leveraging ORMs like SQLAlchemy for more complex database interactions. These tools and techniques are essential for developing applications that manage and manipulate relational data efficiently.

To continue exploring SQLAlchemy, it is essential to understand how it manages database schemas and interactions. SQLAlchemy uses a combination of core and ORM components, each offering different levels of abstraction for working with databases.

In SQLAlchemy's ORM approach, you define database tables as Python classes and their attributes as columns. This method allows you to interact with the database using high-level Python objects rather than writing raw SQL queries. Let's walk through a practical example to see how this works.

First, you'll need to create an `Engine`, which serves as the entry point for the database connection. The `Engine` manages connections to the database and provides a means for executing SQL statements. To define and manage your schema, you'll use `Declarative Base`, which allows you to define tables and mappings between your Python classes and database tables.

Here's how you can set up a basic SQLite database using SQLAlchemy:

```python
from sqlalchemy import create_engine, Column, Integer, String
from sqlalchemy.ext.declarative import declarative_base
from sqlalchemy.orm import sessionmaker

Create an engine that connects to an SQLite database file
engine  create_engine('sqlite:///example.db')

Create a base class for declarative class definitions
Base  declarative_base()

Define a User class that maps to the users table
class User(Base):
    __tablename__  'users'

    id  Column(Integer, primary_keyTrue, autoincrementTrue)
    name  Column(String, nullableFalse)
    email  Column(String, uniqueTrue, nullableFalse)

Create the table in the database
Base.metadata.create_all(engine)

Create a session to interact with the database
Session  sessionmaker(bindengine)
session  Session()

Add a new user to the database
new_user  User(name'John Doe', email'john.doe@example.com')
session.add(new_user)
session.commit()

Query the database
user  session.query(User).filter_by(name'John Doe').first()
print(user.name, user.email)
```

```
Close the session
session.close()
```

In this example, the `User` class is defined with attributes corresponding to columns in the `users` table. The `Base.metadata.create_all(engine)` line creates the table in the SQLite database. The `sessionmaker` function creates a new `Session` object that you use to interact with the database.

CRUD operations are managed through the session object. To create a new record, you instantiate a `User` object and add it to the session. Calling `session.commit()` saves these changes to the database. For reading data, you use the `query` method to retrieve records based on filters. Finally, closing the session ensures that any open resources are released.

SQLAlchemy also supports advanced querying capabilities using its powerful query API. For example, you can perform joins, aggregate functions, and more complex queries using the ORM methods. Here's an example of a more complex query:

```python
from sqlalchemy import func

Query all users and count the total number
users session.query(User).all()
total_users session.query(func.count(User.id)).scalar()
print(f'Total users: {total_users}')
```

This code retrieves all users from the `users` table and calculates the total number of users using SQLAlchemy's `func` module, which provides access to SQL functions.

Handling database migrations is another important aspect of database management. SQLAlchemy provides tools for schema migrations through a library called Alembic. Alembic allows you to version your database schema, apply incremental changes, and manage complex schema evolution scenarios. Installing Alembic via pip is straightforward:

```sh
pip install alembic
```

Once installed, you can initialize an Alembic environment and generate migration scripts to track changes to your database schema. Alembic's integration with SQLAlchemy makes it a valuable tool for managing database schema changes in a production environment.

In summary, interacting with databases using Python involves understanding and using SQL for managing relational data. Libraries like SQLite and SQLAlchemy offer powerful tools for performing CRUD operations, managing transactions, and defining schemas. By leveraging these libraries, you can efficiently handle database interactions and integrate them into your Python applications. Whether working with lightweight SQLite databases or more robust systems managed by SQLAlchemy, these skills are crucial for developing data-driven applications.

CHAPTER 23:

In addition to data cleaning, exploratory data analysis (EDA) is a crucial step in understanding your dataset. EDA involves summarizing the main characteristics of the data, often using visual methods. Pandas provides several built-in functions that facilitate this process, allowing you to gain insights into your data and identify patterns, trends, and anomalies.

One fundamental aspect of EDA is generating summary statistics, which can be easily achieved with the `describe()` method. This method provides a statistical summary of each column in the DataFrame, including measures like mean, standard deviation, minimum, and maximum values, along with quartiles. For example:

```python
import pandas as pd

Sample DataFrame
data {
   'Name': ['Alice', 'Bob', 'Charlie', 'David', 'Eve'],
   'Age': [25, 30, 35, 40, 45],
   'Salary': [50000, 60000, 70000, 80000, 90000]
}
df pd.DataFrame(data)

Generate summary statistics
print(df.describe())
```

The `describe()` method is useful for numeric columns, but for categorical data, you might use methods like `value_counts()`

to get a count of unique values. For instance, if you have a column representing different job titles or categories, you can use `value_counts()` to see how many occurrences there are of each category:

```python
Categorical example
df['Job Title'] ['Engineer', 'Manager', 'Engineer', 'Manager', 'Analyst']
print(df['Job Title'].value_counts())
```

Another important component of EDA is data visualization. While Pandas itself offers some basic plotting capabilities, it is often used in conjunction with libraries such as Matplotlib and Seaborn for more sophisticated visualizations. For instance, to visualize the distribution of a numerical column, you might use a histogram or box plot.

To generate a histogram, you can use the `hist()` method of the DataFrame:

```python
import matplotlib.pyplot as plt

Plot a histogram of the 'Salary' column
df['Salary'].hist()
plt.title('Salary Distribution')
plt.xlabel('Salary')
plt.ylabel('Frequency')
plt.show()
```

Box plots are useful for visualizing the distribution of data and identifying outliers. You can use the `boxplot()` method to create a box plot:

```python
Plot a box plot of the 'Salary' column
```

```
df.boxplot(column'Salary')
plt.title('Salary Box Plot')
plt.ylabel('Salary')
plt.show()
```

Correlation analysis is another key aspect of EDA. It helps in understanding the relationship between different variables. Pandas provides the `corr()` method to compute the pairwise correlation of columns. For example, if you want to see how `Age` correlates with `Salary`, you can do:

```python
Compute correlation matrix
correlation_matrix df.corr()
print(correlation_matrix)
```

This matrix will show the correlation coefficients between each pair of numerical columns, helping you to determine which variables have strong linear relationships with each other.

Pandas also supports handling time series data, which is often encountered in financial analysis, forecasting, and other fields. Time series data in Pandas is managed using `DatetimeIndex` and the `datetime` module. You can easily convert a column to datetime format and set it as the index:

```python
Sample time series data
date_data {
  'Date': pd.date_range(start'2023-01-01', periods5, freq'D'),
  'Value': [100, 200, 150, 300, 250]
}
df pd.DataFrame(date_data)
df.set_index('Date', inplaceTrue)
```

Plot time series data

```
df['Value'].plot()
plt.title('Value Over Time')
plt.xlabel('Date')
plt.ylabel('Value')
plt.show()
```

When working with time series data, you can perform resampling, which involves changing the frequency of the data, such as aggregating daily data to monthly averages. Pandas provides the `resample()` method for this purpose:

```python
Resample to monthly frequency
monthly_data df.resample('M').mean()
print(monthly_data)
```

This method allows you to aggregate data by different time periods, which is essential for analyzing trends over time.

Lastly, Pandas integrates well with other data processing libraries and tools, making it a versatile choice for data analysis tasks. By mastering the fundamental operations with Pandas, you will be well-equipped to handle a variety of data analysis challenges and gain meaningful insights from your data.

Continuing from our discussion on data visualization, the use of scatter plots can also be instrumental when exploring relationships between two continuous variables. In Pandas, the `plot()` method is quite versatile, and with the help of Matplotlib, we can produce scatter plots to visualize these relationships.

Consider a scenario where you want to examine the correlation between 'Age' and 'Salary' in a DataFrame. You can create a scatter plot as follows:

```python
```

```python
import matplotlib.pyplot as plt

Create a scatter plot
df.plot(kind'scatter', x'Age', y'Salary')
plt.title('Age vs Salary')
plt.xlabel('Age')
plt.ylabel('Salary')
plt.show()
```

This plot will allow you to visually assess if there is a trend or pattern between the two variables, such as whether salaries tend to increase with age.

Furthermore, advanced plotting capabilities are available through Seaborn, a library built on top of Matplotlib that integrates seamlessly with Pandas DataFrames. Seaborn provides a high-level interface for drawing attractive and informative statistical graphics. For example, you can use Seaborn to create a pair plot that visualizes pairwise relationships in a dataset. This can be particularly useful for examining correlations and distributions across multiple variables.

```python
import seaborn as sns

Create a pair plot
sns.pairplot(df[['Age', 'Salary']])
plt.show()
```

The `pairplot` function produces a grid of scatter plots for each pair of variables and histograms for each individual variable, giving you a comprehensive view of your dataset's structure.

In addition to visualizing relationships, another critical aspect of data analysis is handling and analyzing time series data. Pandas provides robust tools for working with time series, including functionality for resampling, rolling statistics, and time-based indexing. Suppose you have a dataset with timestamps and want to analyze how a variable changes over time.

```python
Example of creating a time series DataFrame
dates pd.date_range(start'2022-01-01', periods100, freq'D')
data {
  'Date': dates,
  'Value': np.random.randn(100).cumsum()
}
time_series_df pd.DataFrame(data)
time_series_df.set_index('Date', inplaceTrue)

Plotting the time series data
time_series_df.plot()
plt.title('Time Series Data')
plt.xlabel('Date')
plt.ylabel('Value')
plt.show()
```

By setting the 'Date' column as the index, we can leverage Pandas' time series functionalities. For example, resampling data to a different frequency, such as monthly averages, can be accomplished with the `resample()` method:

```python
Resample data to monthly frequency and calculate the mean
monthly_data time_series_df.resample('M').mean()
monthly_data.plot()
plt.title('Monthly Average Value')
plt.xlabel('Date')
plt.ylabel('Average Value')
plt.show()
```

This resampling technique is useful for aggregating data to a desired time period and can help in analyzing long-term trends or seasonality.

In summary, Pandas provides a comprehensive suite of tools for handling data from initial loading and cleaning to in-depth analysis and visualization. By mastering DataFrames, summary statistics, and advanced plotting techniques, you can gain significant insights from your data. Whether you are exploring basic trends or complex relationships, these tools enable you to interpret and visualize data effectively, leading to more informed decision-making and analysis.

CHAPTER 24:

In addition to line and scatter plots, Matplotlib provides various other plot types that are essential for different types of data visualization. For instance, bar plots are particularly useful for displaying categorical data. To create a bar plot, you would use the `bar()` function from the `pyplot` module. Here's how you can generate a bar plot:

```python
categories ['A', 'B', 'C', 'D']
values [10, 20, 15, 25]

plt.bar(categories, values)
plt.xlabel('Categories')
plt.ylabel('Values')
plt.title('Bar Plot Example')
plt.show()
```

This code snippet produces a vertical bar plot where each bar represents a category and its corresponding value. The `bar()` function is versatile and can be customized to produce horizontal bar plots using the `barh()` function. Customization options include adjusting the color, edge color, and width of the bars.

Another important type of plot is the histogram, which is used to represent the distribution of numerical data. Histograms are created using the `hist()` function. For example, if you have a list of numerical data points and you want to visualize their distribution, you would use:

```python
data [1, 2, 2, 3, 4, 4, 4, 5, 6, 7, 8, 9, 10]

plt.hist(data, bins5, edgecolor'black')
plt.xlabel('Bins')
plt.ylabel('Frequency')
plt.title('Histogram Example')
plt.show()
```

In this example, `bins` parameter specifies the number of bins or intervals into which the data is divided. Histograms are useful for understanding the frequency distribution of a dataset, and adjusting the number of bins can help reveal different patterns in the data.

Pie charts are another visualization tool used to show proportions of a whole. They are especially useful when you want to display relative percentages or fractions. To create a pie chart, you use the `pie()` function. Consider the following example:

```python
sizes [30, 20, 10, 40]
labels ['A', 'B', 'C', 'D']

plt.pie(sizes, labelslabels, autopct'%1.1f%%', startangle140)
plt.title('Pie Chart Example')
plt.show()
```

Here, `autopct` parameter formats the percentage labels on the pie slices, and `startangle` rotates the start of the pie chart to improve readability. Pie charts provide a visual impression of the proportion of each category, which can be useful for displaying categorical data with a clear representation of parts to a whole.

Matplotlib also supports more complex visualizations such as 3D plots, which can be particularly useful for visualizing three-dimensional data. To create 3D plots, you need to import the `Axes3D` class from `mpl_toolkits.mplot3d`. Here's a basic example of a 3D scatter plot:

```python
from mpl_toolkits.mplot3d import Axes3D
import numpy as np

fig plt.figure()
ax fig.add_subplot(111, projection'3d')

x np.random.rand(100)
y np.random.rand(100)
z np.random.rand(100)

ax.scatter(x, y, z)
ax.set_xlabel('X Label')
ax.set_ylabel('Y Label')
ax.set_zlabel('Z Label')
plt.title('3D Scatter Plot Example')
plt.show()
```

In this example, random values are generated for the x, y, and z coordinates, and the `scatter()` function creates a 3D scatter plot. The `set_xlabel()`, `set_ylabel()`, and `set_zlabel()` functions label the axes of the 3D plot. This type of plot is valuable when dealing with multidimensional data and requires visualization of data points in three dimensions.

Matplotlib's flexibility extends to customizing plots extensively. You can modify plot elements such as line styles, markers, colors, and axis properties. For example, to customize a line plot, you can specify line styles and markers as follows:

```python
```

```
x [1, 2, 3, 4, 5]
y [1, 4, 9, 16, 25]

plt.plot(x, y, linestyle'--', marker'o', color'b')
plt.xlabel('X-axis Label')
plt.ylabel('Y-axis Label')
plt.title('Customized Line Plot')
plt.show()
```

Here, `linestyle'--'` specifies a dashed line, `marker'o'` adds circular markers at each data point, and `color'b'` sets the line color to blue. These customization options allow you to tailor visualizations to meet specific needs and preferences.

Incorporating visualizations into data analysis involves not only creating plots but also ensuring that they effectively communicate insights. This means choosing the appropriate type of plot for your data, customizing visual elements for clarity, and integrating plots into reports or presentations as needed. As you work with Matplotlib, you will find that practice and experimentation with different plot types and customization options will enhance your ability to convey data-driven insights effectively.

The `pie()` function is highly customizable. For instance, you can modify the colors of the segments by using the `colors` parameter, and adjust the appearance of the wedges by using the `explode` parameter to pull a slice out from the pie, which can emphasize specific portions of the data. Here's an example of a customized pie chart:

```python
sizes [30, 20, 10, 40]
labels ['A', 'B', 'C', 'D']
colors ['gold', 'yellowgreen', 'lightcoral', 'lightskyblue']
explode (0.1, 0, 0, 0)  explode the 1st slice
```

```python
plt.pie(sizes, labelslabels, colorscolors, explodeexplode, autopct'%1.1f%%', shadowTrue, startangle140)
plt.title('Customized Pie Chart Example')
plt.show()
```

The `scatter()` function, which was briefly mentioned earlier, is instrumental in displaying relationships between two continuous variables. You can enhance scatter plots by adjusting marker styles, colors, and sizes. For instance, if you have data with additional dimensions or categories, you can use different colors or shapes to represent different groups. Here's how to do it:

```python
x [1, 2, 3, 4, 5]
y [2, 3, 4, 5, 6]
sizes [20, 50, 80, 200, 500]
colors [0, 1, 2, 3, 4]

plt.scatter(x, y, ssizes, ccolors, cmap'viridis', alpha0.7, edgecolors'w', linewidth0.5)
plt.xlabel('X-axis')
plt.ylabel('Y-axis')
plt.title('Scatter Plot with Customizations')
plt.colorbar(label'Color Scale')
plt.show()
```

In this scatter plot, `s` controls the size of the markers, and `c` controls their color. The `cmap` parameter specifies the colormap used to translate numerical values into colors, and `alpha` controls the transparency of the markers.

Bar plots, histograms, and pie charts are not the only types of visualizations that Matplotlib offers. Box plots, for instance, are useful for showing the distribution of data through quartiles and identifying potential outliers. Creating a box plot is done using the `boxplot()` function:

```python
data [1, 2, 5, 6, 8, 12, 18, 22, 24, 30, 35, 40]

plt.boxplot(data, vertFalse, patch_artistTrue)
plt.xlabel('Values')
plt.title('Box Plot Example')
plt.show()
```

Box plots provide a summary of a dataset, including the median, quartiles, and potential outliers, which helps in understanding the spread and skewness of the data.

For a more complex dataset, where you might want to compare multiple distributions, `subplot()` becomes invaluable. This function allows for creating multiple plots within a single figure, each showing different aspects of the data. Here's an example of using subplots:

```python
fig, axs plt.subplots(2, 2, figsize(10, 8))

axs[0, 0].plot(x, y, 'r-')
axs[0, 0].set_title('Line Plot')

axs[0, 1].bar(categories, values)
axs[0, 1].set_title('Bar Plot')

axs[1, 0].hist(data, bins5)
axs[1, 0].set_title('Histogram')

axs[1, 1].boxplot(data, vertFalse)
axs[1, 1].set_title('Box Plot')

for ax in axs.flat:
  ax.label_outer()

plt.tight_layout()
```

plt.show()
```

In this example, `fig, axs plt.subplots(2, 2)` creates a 2x2 grid of subplots within a single figure. Each subplot can be customized individually, and the `tight_layout()` function adjusts the spacing between plots for a clean appearance.

Matplotlib also supports advanced features such as 3D plotting using the `mpl_toolkits.mplot3d` module. To create a 3D plot, you would first need to import the `Axes3D` module and then create a 3D figure and axes. For example:

```python
from mpl_toolkits.mplot3d import Axes3D
fig plt.figure()
ax fig.add_subplot(111, projection'3d')

x [1, 2, 3, 4, 5]
y [2, 3, 4, 5, 6]
z [1, 4, 9, 16, 25]

ax.scatter(x, y, z, c'r', marker'o')
ax.set_xlabel('X Label')
ax.set_ylabel('Y Label')
ax.set_zlabel('Z Label')
ax.set_title('3D Scatter Plot')

plt.show()
```

This code snippet illustrates how to generate a 3D scatter plot with labels for each axis. 3D plots are valuable for visualizing data that has three dimensions, allowing for a more comprehensive understanding of relationships between variables.

Throughout the process of creating and customizing plots with Matplotlib, it is essential to remain mindful of clarity and
```

readability. Ensure that your visualizations accurately represent the data and that all labels, titles, and legends are clear and descriptive. The goal of data visualization is not only to present data but to make it easier to understand and interpret.

As you become more proficient with Matplotlib, you will be able to tailor your visualizations to better communicate insights and patterns in your data, making your analyses more effective and impactful.

CHAPTER 25:

Moving beyond supervised learning, unsupervised learning involves training a model on data that has no labeled responses. The primary goal here is to identify patterns or groupings within the data. Unlike supervised learning, where the outcomes are known and the model learns to predict these outcomes, unsupervised learning is concerned with exploring the structure of data without predefined categories. This can include clustering, where the algorithm attempts to group similar data points together, or dimensionality reduction, where the goal is to simplify the data while preserving its essential features.

Clustering is one of the most common unsupervised learning tasks. A popular algorithm for clustering is k-means. K-means clustering partitions the data into k distinct, non-overlapping subsets or clusters. The algorithm assigns each data point to the cluster with the nearest mean value (the centroid), and then recalculates the centroids based on the new assignments. This process is repeated iteratively until the centroids no longer change significantly, indicating that the algorithm has converged. K-means is particularly useful in scenarios where the number of clusters is known beforehand, but it may struggle with clusters of varying sizes or shapes.

Another notable clustering technique is hierarchical clustering, which builds a hierarchy of clusters either through a bottom-up or top-down approach. In agglomerative (bottom-up) hierarchical clustering, each data point starts in its own cluster, and pairs of clusters are merged as one moves up the hierarchy.

Conversely, in divisive (top-down) hierarchical clustering, all data points start in a single cluster, which is progressively split into smaller clusters. The result is a dendrogram, a tree-like diagram that shows the arrangement of the clusters. Hierarchical clustering can be more flexible than k-means but is computationally more intensive, especially with large datasets.

Dimensionality reduction is another important aspect of unsupervised learning, aimed at reducing the number of features in a dataset while retaining as much information as possible. Principal Component Analysis (PCA) is a widely used method for this purpose. PCA works by identifying the directions (principal components) along which the variance of the data is maximized. By projecting the data onto these principal components, PCA reduces the number of dimensions while maintaining the core structure of the data. This technique is valuable for visualizing high-dimensional data and improving the performance of other machine learning algorithms by eliminating noise and redundancy.

Feature selection and extraction are closely related to dimensionality reduction. Feature selection involves choosing a subset of relevant features from the original dataset, while feature extraction involves transforming the data into a new set of features. Both methods aim to improve model performance and interpretability by reducing the dimensionality of the data.

Evaluation of machine learning models is crucial to understanding their effectiveness and ensuring their reliability. The evaluation process involves assessing the model's performance using various metrics and validation techniques. For supervised learning, common metrics include accuracy, precision, recall, and F1 score. Accuracy measures the proportion of correctly classified instances, while precision and recall evaluate the model's performance in identifying positive instances. The F1 score is the harmonic mean of precision and recall, providing a single metric that balances both aspects.

In addition to these metrics, cross-validation is an essential technique for evaluating model performance. Cross-validation involves partitioning the dataset into multiple subsets or folds, training the model on some of these folds, and testing it on the remaining folds. This process is repeated multiple times to ensure that the model is tested on different subsets of the data, providing a more robust estimate of its performance.

For unsupervised learning, evaluation can be more challenging due to the absence of labeled outcomes. In clustering tasks, metrics such as silhouette score and Davies-Bouldin index can be used to assess the quality of the clusters. These metrics evaluate how well-separated and compact the clusters are, helping to determine the optimal number of clusters and the effectiveness of the clustering algorithm.

Understanding these foundational concepts in machine learning lays the groundwork for more advanced techniques and applications. As we explore more complex models and algorithms in subsequent discussions, the principles of supervised and unsupervised learning, along with effective evaluation methods, will be essential in guiding the development and deployment of machine learning solutions.

When it comes to evaluating model performance, understanding the effectiveness of a machine learning model is crucial. This involves assessing how well the model generalizes to unseen data. To evaluate model performance, we use various metrics that depend on the type of learning task. For supervised learning, common metrics include accuracy, precision, recall, F1 score, and the ROC curve.

Accuracy measures the proportion of correctly classified instances out of the total number of instances. While it provides a straightforward evaluation of a model's performance, accuracy can be misleading in cases of imbalanced datasets where one class significantly outnumbers the other. For instance, in a dataset where 95% of instances belong to one class, a model that always predicts the majority class would still achieve high accuracy, despite not being useful.

Precision and recall offer more nuanced insights, particularly in imbalanced datasets. Precision, also known as positive predictive value, measures the proportion of true positive predictions among all positive predictions made by the model. In contrast, recall, or sensitivity, measures the proportion of true positive predictions among all actual positives in the dataset. The F1 score is the harmonic mean of precision and recall, providing a single metric that balances the trade-off between them. This is especially useful when the cost of false positives and false negatives varies.

For binary classification tasks, the Receiver Operating Characteristic (ROC) curve is an essential tool. The ROC curve plots the true positive rate (recall) against the false positive rate at various threshold settings. The area under the ROC curve (AUC) quantifies the model's ability to discriminate between positive and negative classes, with a higher AUC indicating better performance.

In unsupervised learning, performance evaluation can be more challenging due to the lack of ground truth labels. For clustering algorithms like k-means, internal metrics such as the Silhouette Score and Davies-Bouldin Index help assess the quality of the clusters. The Silhouette Score measures how similar an instance is to its own cluster compared to other clusters, providing a way to evaluate how well-separated the clusters are. The Davies-Bouldin Index calculates the average similarity ratio of each cluster with its most similar cluster, aiming for a lower score indicating better clustering quality.

In the realm of dimensionality reduction, the effectiveness of techniques like PCA is often evaluated based on how well the reduced dimensions capture the variance of the original data.

Variance explained by principal components is a key metric; typically, we seek to retain a high percentage of the total variance while reducing the number of dimensions. This allows us to ensure that the reduced feature space still contains most of the original information, facilitating further analysis or improving the performance of subsequent machine learning models.

Moreover, cross-validation is a robust technique used to assess model performance more reliably. Cross-validation involves partitioning the dataset into multiple folds, training the model on a subset of these folds, and validating it on the remaining fold. This process is repeated several times with different partitions, providing a comprehensive evaluation of the model's performance across different subsets of the data. Common methods include k-fold cross-validation, where the data is divided into k subsets, and leave-one-out cross-validation, where each instance is used once as the validation set while the remaining instances form the training set.

Hyperparameter tuning is another aspect that significantly influences model performance. Many machine learning algorithms come with parameters that need to be set before training begins, such as the number of clusters in k-means or the regularization strength in linear regression. Hyperparameter tuning involves finding the optimal values for these parameters to improve model performance. Techniques like grid search and randomized search can automate this process, systematically evaluating different combinations of hyperparameters to identify the most effective ones.

Finally, it is essential to recognize the importance of domain knowledge in both model development and evaluation. Understanding the context of the data and the problem at hand helps in selecting appropriate algorithms, defining relevant metrics, and interpreting results accurately. For instance, in a healthcare application, false negatives (e.g., missing a disease diagnosis) might be more critical than false positives, affecting the choice of evaluation metrics and model tuning strategies.

By integrating these practices, one can effectively harness the power of machine learning, developing models that not only perform well on training data but also generalize effectively to new, unseen data. As we continue to explore and apply these techniques, the ability to interpret and validate machine learning models becomes an invaluable skill, driving better decision-making and more insightful data analysis.

CHAPTER 26:

As we advance in using Scikit-Learn for building machine learning models, it's crucial to delve into hyperparameter tuning, which plays a pivotal role in enhancing model performance. Hyperparameters are configurations external to the model that are set before the learning process begins. They control the learning process and affect the model's ability to generalize well to new, unseen data. Unlike parameters, which are learned during the training phase, hyperparameters must be tuned manually or through systematic search methods.

Scikit-Learn provides several techniques for hyperparameter tuning. One common method is grid search, which exhaustively tests a predefined set of hyperparameters to find the best combination. The `GridSearchCV` class is used for this purpose. It performs an exhaustive search over a specified parameter grid and evaluates each combination using cross-validation. For instance, if you are tuning a Support Vector Machine (SVM) model, you might want to adjust parameters like the regularization parameter `C` and the kernel type. The `GridSearchCV` class would test different values for these parameters and select the combination that yields the best performance based on a specified scoring metric.

Another effective method is random search, implemented through the `RandomizedSearchCV` class. Unlike grid search, random search randomly samples a specified number of hyperparameter combinations from a defined distribution. This approach can be more efficient, especially when dealing with a large number of hyperparameters or a vast parameter space.

By setting a fixed number of iterations, random search can provide a good balance between search space exploration and computational efficiency.

After hyperparameter tuning, the next step is model validation. Validation involves assessing how well the model performs on unseen data to ensure that it generalizes well beyond the training set. Scikit-Learn offers several techniques for model validation, with cross-validation being one of the most widely used methods. Cross-validation involves dividing the dataset into multiple folds and training the model on different subsets of the data while validating it on the remaining folds. This process helps to provide a more reliable estimate of the model's performance.

The `cross_val_score` function in Scikit-Learn simplifies this process by performing cross-validation and returning the scores for each fold. For example, if you use five-fold cross-validation, the function will return an array of five scores, each representing the model's performance on one of the validation folds. These scores can be averaged to obtain a more stable estimate of the model's performance.

In addition to cross-validation, Scikit-Learn provides tools for assessing model performance through various metrics. For classification tasks, metrics such as accuracy, precision, recall, F1 score, and the ROC-AUC score offer valuable insights into how well the model performs. Accuracy measures the overall correctness of the model, while precision and recall provide insights into the model's performance with respect to specific classes. The F1 score combines precision and recall into a single metric, and the ROC-AUC score evaluates the model's ability to distinguish between classes.

For regression tasks, metrics such as mean squared error (MSE), mean absolute error (MAE), and R-squared are commonly used. MSE measures the average squared difference between predicted and actual values, while MAE calculates the average absolute difference. R-squared represents the proportion of variance in the dependent variable that is predictable from the independent variables.

Integrating Scikit-Learn models into a data analysis workflow involves leveraging these tools effectively to build robust machine learning solutions. After selecting and tuning a model, you may need to deploy it for real-world applications. Scikit-Learn supports this process through serialization and deserialization of models. The `joblib` library, which is compatible with Scikit-Learn, allows you to save trained models to disk and load them for future use.

For example, you can use the `joblib.dump` function to save a trained model and `joblib.load` to load it back into memory. This functionality is essential for deploying machine learning models in production environments, where they can be used to make predictions on new data.

By following these steps and utilizing Scikit-Learn's extensive features, you can effectively build, tune, and validate machine learning models. The library's simplicity and flexibility make it a powerful tool for both beginners and experienced practitioners in the field of machine learning. Through hands-on experience with real-world datasets, you will develop a deeper understanding of the modeling process and gain valuable skills for applying machine learning techniques to various problems.

Once you have fine-tuned your hyperparameters and validated your model, the next critical step is to assess and interpret the results to ensure that the model not only performs well but also provides actionable insights. This involves several tasks, including evaluating performance metrics, analyzing confusion matrices, and understanding feature importance.

Evaluating performance metrics is essential for understanding how well your model is likely to perform on new, unseen data. Scikit-Learn offers a variety of metrics to evaluate model performance, depending on the type of problem you are solving. For classification tasks, metrics such as accuracy, precision, recall, and F1-score provide a comprehensive view of how well the model classifies data into categories. Accuracy measures the proportion of correctly classified instances out of the total, while precision and recall offer insights into the model's performance on specific classes. The F1-score combines precision and recall into a single metric, providing a balanced measure of a model's performance.

For regression problems, where the goal is to predict continuous values, metrics such as Mean Absolute Error (MAE), Mean Squared Error (MSE), and R-squared (R^2) are commonly used. MAE measures the average absolute difference between predicted and actual values, giving an idea of the average error magnitude. MSE, on the other hand, penalizes larger errors more heavily due to its squared nature, providing a measure that can be more sensitive to outliers. R-squared explains the proportion of variance in the dependent variable that is predictable from the independent variables, indicating how well the model fits the data.

In addition to performance metrics, analyzing confusion matrices for classification models is invaluable. A confusion matrix displays the counts of true positives, true negatives, false positives, and false negatives, offering a detailed view of how well the model is classifying each class. Scikit-Learn's `confusion_matrix` function generates this matrix, which can then be visualized using heatmaps for more intuitive understanding. The matrix helps identify which classes are being misclassified and provides insights into potential areas for improvement.

Understanding feature importance is another crucial aspect of model interpretation. In many machine learning models, especially tree-based algorithms like Random Forests and Gradient Boosting, feature importance scores can indicate which features most significantly impact the model's predictions. Scikit-Learn provides the `feature_importances_` attribute in these models, allowing you to extract and visualize feature importance. This information can guide feature selection and engineering processes, helping to refine the model by focusing on the most impactful features.

Finally, deploying a machine learning model is often the end goal of the model-building process. Deployment involves integrating the trained model into a production environment where it can make predictions on new data. Scikit-Learn models can be saved and loaded using Python's `pickle` module or joblib library. This allows you to serialize the model into a file and deserialize it later for prediction or further analysis. For deployment, it is also important to consider aspects such as scaling, monitoring, and maintaining the model, ensuring that it continues to perform well as new data becomes available.

Through practical examples and hands-on experience, working with Scikit-Learn empowers you to build, evaluate, and deploy machine learning models effectively. By mastering model training, hyperparameter tuning, validation, and interpretation, you gain the ability to harness the power of machine learning in real-world applications, deriving actionable insights and making data-driven decisions.

CHAPTER 27:

To further explore the core aspects of neural networks, we must also address the concept of backpropagation and optimization algorithms, which are integral to training deep learning models. Backpropagation is the method used to update the weights of the network based on the error between the predicted output and the actual target values. This process involves calculating the gradient of the loss function with respect to each weight by applying the chain rule of calculus. TensorFlow facilitates this process through its automatic differentiation capabilities, which allow for efficient computation of gradients and updates during training.

In TensorFlow, the training of a neural network involves defining a loss function, selecting an optimization algorithm, and iterating over the data in multiple epochs to minimize the loss function. The loss function quantifies the difference between the predicted output and the true labels, and common loss functions include Mean Squared Error (MSE) for regression tasks and Categorical Crossentropy for classification tasks. TensorFlow offers a range of built-in loss functions through its `tf.keras.losses` module, which can be easily integrated into model training.

Optimization algorithms are used to adjust the weights of the network to minimize the loss function. The most common optimization algorithm is Stochastic Gradient Descent (SGD), which updates the weights based on the gradient of the loss function with respect to the weights. Variants of SGD, such as Momentum, Adagrad, and Adam, are also frequently used to enhance training performance. Adam, in particular, is popular due to its adaptive learning rate and momentum-based updates, which often lead to faster convergence. TensorFlow's `tf.keras.optimizers` module provides implementations of these optimization algorithms, allowing users to select the most suitable one for their specific task.

In practical applications, deep learning models are frequently employed for image recognition tasks. Convolutional Neural Networks (CNNs) are a class of neural networks specifically designed for this purpose. CNNs utilize convolutional layers to automatically and adaptively learn spatial hierarchies of features from input images. These layers apply convolutional filters to the input image, producing feature maps that capture various aspects of the image, such as edges, textures, and patterns. Pooling layers, such as Max Pooling, are then used to reduce the dimensionality of these feature maps while retaining the most important information.

To implement a CNN in TensorFlow, one would typically start by defining the convolutional layers using `tf.keras.layers.Conv2D`, followed by activation functions like ReLU and pooling layers using `tf.keras.layers.MaxPooling2D`. After several convolutional and pooling layers, the output is flattened and passed through one or more fully connected (Dense) layers before producing the final classification or regression output. TensorFlow's `tf.keras.Sequential` API allows for straightforward construction of such models by stacking layers in sequence.

Natural Language Processing (NLP) is another area where deep learning models have shown significant advancements. Recurrent Neural Networks (RNNs) and Long Short-Term Memory (LSTM) networks are commonly used for sequential data tasks such as text classification and language modeling. RNNs are designed to handle sequences of varying lengths by maintaining a hidden state that evolves over time. LSTMs, an extension of RNNs, address the limitations of traditional RNNs in capturing long-range dependencies by incorporating mechanisms to manage the flow of information through gates, effectively mitigating issues like vanishing gradients.

In TensorFlow, RNNs and LSTMs can be implemented using `tf.keras.layers.SimpleRNN` and `tf.keras.layers.LSTM`, respectively. These layers can be used to process sequences of text or time-series data. For text data, it is common to preprocess the text using tokenization and embedding layers. The `tf.keras.layers.Embedding` layer converts text sequences into dense vector representations, which are then fed into the RNN or LSTM layers for further processing. The output can be used for tasks such as sentiment analysis or machine translation.

In addition to the core functionalities provided by TensorFlow, there are numerous tools and techniques for improving model performance and efficiency. Techniques such as dropout, which involves randomly setting a fraction of input units to zero during training, help prevent overfitting by ensuring that the model does not rely too heavily on any single neuron. Batch normalization is another technique used to stabilize and accelerate training by normalizing the inputs of each layer.

To summarize, TensorFlow offers a robust and flexible framework for building and training deep learning models. By understanding neural network architectures, activation functions, optimization algorithms, and specific techniques for tasks like image recognition and NLP, one can harness the power of deep learning to solve a wide range of complex problems. Through hands-on practice with TensorFlow, one gains practical experience in implementing and fine-tuning deep learning models, which is crucial for advancing in the field of machine learning.

To effectively deploy deep learning models, understanding and implementing techniques for evaluating and fine-tuning these models is essential. Evaluation metrics help assess the performance of the model and guide adjustments to improve its accuracy and robustness. For classification tasks, metrics such as accuracy, precision, recall, and F1-score are crucial. Accuracy measures the proportion of correctly classified instances, while precision and recall provide insights into the model's performance on positive and negative classes, respectively. The F1-score combines precision and recall into a single metric, which is particularly useful in scenarios where class imbalance exists.

For regression tasks, metrics such as Mean Absolute Error (MAE), Mean Squared Error (MSE), and Root Mean Squared Error (RMSE) are commonly used. MAE measures the average magnitude of errors in predictions, MSE emphasizes larger errors due to its squaring operation, and RMSE provides a measure of error in the same units as the target variable. TensorFlow provides built-in functions for these metrics, allowing for straightforward evaluation of model performance during training and testing phases.

Hyperparameter tuning is a critical aspect of model optimization. Hyperparameters are parameters that are set before the training process begins, such as the number of layers in a neural network, the number of units in each layer, the learning rate, and the batch size. Tuning these hyperparameters can significantly impact the model's performance. Techniques such as grid search, random search, and more advanced methods like Bayesian optimization are used to explore different combinations of hyperparameters. TensorFlow's integration with tools like Keras Tuner simplifies the process of hyperparameter tuning by automating the search process and providing insights into the best configurations.

Another important aspect of training deep learning models is dealing with overfitting and underfitting. Overfitting occurs when a model learns the training data too well, including noise and anomalies, leading to poor generalization to new, unseen data. Underfitting, on the other hand, happens when the model fails to capture the underlying patterns in the data, resulting in poor performance on both training and test datasets. Techniques to address overfitting include regularization methods such as L1 and L2 regularization, dropout, and early stopping. Regularization adds a penalty to the loss function to prevent the model from fitting the noise, while dropout randomly omits neurons during training to improve generalization. Early stopping involves monitoring the model's performance on a validation set and stopping training when performance ceases to improve.

For handling text data, Recurrent Neural Networks (RNNs) and their more advanced variants, such as Long Short-Term Memory (LSTM) networks and Gated Recurrent Units (GRUs), are commonly used. RNNs are designed to process sequences of data by maintaining a hidden state that captures information from previous time steps. LSTMs and GRUs improve upon traditional RNNs by incorporating mechanisms to better capture long-term dependencies and mitigate issues such as vanishing gradients. TensorFlow provides modules to easily construct and train RNNs, LSTMs, and GRUs, facilitating the implementation of models for tasks like sentiment analysis, language modeling, and sequence prediction.

To summarize, TensorFlow is a powerful library that simplifies the implementation of deep learning models, from defining network architectures and training models to evaluating performance and fine-tuning hyperparameters. Understanding the fundamentals of neural network architecture, activation functions, loss functions, optimization algorithms, and evaluation metrics equips practitioners with the tools necessary to build effective deep learning models. By leveraging TensorFlow's comprehensive suite of features and its ecosystem of tools, one can address a wide range of problems in fields such as computer vision and natural language processing, driving advancements in artificial intelligence and machine learning.

CHAPTER 28:

In addition to choosing the right cloud deployment model, you must consider how to set up and manage your web servers. Web servers are crucial for hosting web applications and ensuring they are accessible over the internet. Popular web servers include Nginx and Apache, which are often used in combination with web application frameworks like Flask or Django to serve Python applications.

When configuring a web server for deployment, the primary task is to ensure that it can properly interface with your application. This typically involves setting up a reverse proxy, which allows the web server to forward incoming requests to your Python application running on a specific port. For example, Nginx can be configured to handle HTTP requests and then pass them to a Gunicorn server running your Flask or Django application. This setup not only optimizes request handling but also provides additional layers of security and scalability.

Managing deployments involves more than just setting up web servers and cloud infrastructure. It requires implementing robust deployment workflows and ensuring that your application is continuously available and performing well. Continuous Integration/Continuous Deployment (CI/CD) pipelines are a key aspect of this process. CI/CD pipelines automate the testing, building, and deployment of your application, facilitating frequent and reliable releases. Tools such as Jenkins, GitLab CI, and GitHub Actions can be used to create and manage these pipelines, ensuring that each update to your codebase is automatically tested and deployed.

Another important aspect of managing deployments is monitoring and logging. Monitoring tools track the performance and health of your application, alerting you to potential issues before they affect users. Popular monitoring solutions include Prometheus, Grafana, and New Relic. These tools can help you track metrics such as response times, error rates, and resource usage, allowing you to make informed decisions about scaling and optimization.

Logging provides a record of application activity and errors, which is invaluable for debugging and understanding user behavior. Log management systems like ELK Stack (Elasticsearch, Logstash, Kibana) and Splunk aggregate and analyze logs from various sources, offering insights into the operation and performance of your application. Properly configured logging can help you quickly identify and resolve issues, improving the reliability and user experience of your application.

Security is another critical consideration when deploying applications. Ensuring that your deployment environment is secure involves implementing practices such as setting up firewalls, encrypting data, and regularly updating dependencies. For web applications, using HTTPS to encrypt data transmitted between users and your server is essential. Additionally, keeping your server and application dependencies up to date helps protect against vulnerabilities and exploits.

As you prepare for deployment, it is also essential to plan for scaling and load management. Depending on your application's usage patterns, you might need to handle increased traffic by scaling your infrastructure. Horizontal scaling, where you add more instances of your application, and vertical scaling, where you increase the resources of existing instances, are common approaches. Cloud platforms often provide auto-scaling features that automatically adjust the number of running instances based on traffic and load, ensuring that your application remains responsive and available during peak times.

In summary, deploying Python applications requires a comprehensive approach that includes preparing your application for production, utilizing containerization with Docker, selecting and configuring cloud services and web servers, and managing deployments through CI/CD pipelines. Effective deployment also involves monitoring, logging, and securing your application, as well as planning for scaling to handle varying loads. By addressing these aspects, you can ensure that your Python projects are successfully transitioned from development to a live, operational state, providing a seamless experience for your users and maintaining the reliability of your application.

In addition to the technical aspects of deploying applications, managing configurations and updates is a crucial element of ensuring smooth operation and minimal downtime. Configuration management tools like Ansible, Chef, and Puppet can automate the process of setting up and maintaining the required environments for your application. These tools allow you to define your infrastructure as code, making it easier to replicate setups, enforce consistency, and quickly deploy changes across multiple environments.

As you prepare your Python application for production, it is essential to focus on scalability. Scalability ensures that your application can handle increased loads without degradation in performance. Horizontal scaling, which involves adding more instances of your application to distribute the load, is often used in conjunction with load balancers. A load balancer directs incoming traffic to various instances of your application, ensuring that no single instance becomes overwhelmed. Popular load balancers include HAProxy and Nginx.

Vertical scaling, on the other hand, involves upgrading the hardware resources of a single instance, such as adding more

CPU or memory. While vertical scaling can be beneficial for applications with specific performance needs, it often has limitations compared to horizontal scaling, particularly in terms of fault tolerance and resource limits.

To further enhance scalability and resilience, consider incorporating a microservices architecture into your deployment strategy. Microservices break down an application into smaller, independent services that can be developed, deployed, and scaled individually. This approach allows for more flexible and efficient management of application components. Container orchestration platforms like Kubernetes are particularly useful for managing microservices deployments, as they automate the deployment, scaling, and operation of containers across a cluster of machines.

Data management is another critical aspect of deployment. When deploying applications that rely on databases or other data stores, it is important to ensure that these components are properly managed and secured. This involves setting up automated backups, ensuring data integrity, and implementing proper access controls. Additionally, using managed database services offered by cloud providers, such as Amazon RDS or Google Cloud SQL, can simplify database management and reduce operational overhead.

Testing is an integral part of preparing your application for deployment. Comprehensive testing strategies, including unit tests, integration tests, and end-to-end tests, ensure that your application functions correctly and meets user requirements. Automated testing frameworks like pytest or unittest can be integrated into your CI/CD pipelines to catch issues early in the development process and maintain high code quality.

Finally, post-deployment monitoring and maintenance are essential for maintaining application health and user satisfaction. After your application is live, it is important to continuously monitor its performance and reliability. Implementing alerting systems for critical metrics and logs allows you to respond quickly to any issues that arise. Regular maintenance tasks, such as updating dependencies, applying security patches, and optimizing performance, help keep your application running smoothly and securely over time.

By combining these deployment practices—containerization, cloud services, web server configuration, configuration management, scalability strategies, microservices architecture, data management, rigorous testing, and ongoing maintenance —you can effectively manage the deployment of Python applications. These practices not only ensure that your applications are accessible and performant but also provide a robust foundation for future enhancements and scalability.

CHAPTER 29:

As we continue to explore advanced topics and emerging trends in Python programming, it is imperative to delve into the transformative technologies that are redefining the boundaries of computational possibilities. One significant trend is the rise of edge computing, a paradigm that shifts computation and data storage closer to the location where it is needed, often at or near the source of data generation. This approach reduces latency and bandwidth usage, making it particularly valuable for applications requiring real-time processing, such as autonomous vehicles, IoT devices, and smart cities.

Python plays a crucial role in edge computing through its lightweight nature and support for a variety of platforms. Libraries such as TensorFlow Lite and PyTorch Mobile are designed for deploying machine learning models on mobile and edge devices. These tools help developers create efficient models that can run on devices with limited computational resources. The ability to execute complex computations locally, rather than relying on distant cloud servers, enhances the responsiveness and efficiency of edge applications. As the number of edge devices continues to grow, Python's adaptability and extensive ecosystem will likely drive further innovations in this space.

Another significant advancement is the development of advanced natural language processing (NLP) models. NLP has seen remarkable progress with the advent of models like GPT-4 and BERT, which leverage deep learning techniques to understand and generate human language with unprecedented accuracy. Python's role in NLP is well-supported by libraries such as Hugging Face's Transformers, which provides a wide range of pre-trained models for various NLP tasks including text classification, translation, and summarization. These models, built upon complex neural network architectures, require substantial computational resources and sophisticated tuning to achieve optimal performance. Python facilitates this by offering high-level abstractions and interfaces that simplify the training and deployment of such models. As NLP technology evolves, Python will continue to be a key tool in advancing these capabilities.

Moreover, the integration of Python with data science and analytics is set to expand with the growing emphasis on data-driven decision-making. The proliferation of big data has led to the development of more sophisticated analytics tools and techniques. Python libraries such as Pandas, Dask, and Vaex are enhancing data manipulation and analysis capabilities, allowing for efficient handling of large datasets. These tools enable data scientists to perform complex data operations, from data wrangling and cleaning to exploratory analysis and visualization. The evolution of Python libraries to support larger datasets and more complex analyses reflects the increasing importance of data science in various industries.

In addition to technological advancements, the community-driven evolution of Python contributes significantly to its future trajectory. The Python community, through forums, conferences, and open-source contributions, actively shapes the direction of the language and its ecosystem. The Python Enhancement Proposal (PEP) process is a testament to this collaborative effort, allowing developers to propose and discuss changes to the language. The introduction of new features and improvements, driven by community feedback and technological needs, ensures that Python remains relevant and adaptable to emerging trends.

Furthermore, the rise of interdisciplinary research and

development highlights Python's versatility and growing influence across various fields. From bioinformatics and computational chemistry to financial modeling and social sciences, Python's applicability in diverse domains underscores its role as a universal tool for scientific and industrial applications. This cross-disciplinary integration is facilitated by Python's extensive library ecosystem and its ability to interface with other programming languages and technologies.

As Python continues to evolve, staying updated with the latest developments and trends becomes crucial. Engaging with the Python community, contributing to open-source projects, and participating in professional development opportunities are effective ways to remain at the forefront of technological advancements. Resources such as Python conferences, webinars, and industry publications provide valuable insights into emerging trends and best practices.

In summary, the landscape of Python programming is continuously expanding, driven by advancements in quantum computing, ethical AI, edge computing, NLP, data science, and community-driven evolution. The ability to adapt to these changes and leverage Python's capabilities will be essential for anyone involved in the field. By embracing these trends and staying informed about the latest developments, Python developers can effectively contribute to and benefit from the ongoing evolution of technology.

In the realm of advanced Python programming, the exploration of quantum computing represents a cutting-edge development that promises to revolutionize computational capabilities. Quantum computing leverages the principles of quantum mechanics to process information in fundamentally different ways compared to classical computing. While classical computers use bits as the smallest unit of information, quantum computers use quantum bits or qubits, which can exist in multiple states simultaneously due to superposition.

This property allows quantum computers to handle complex computations more efficiently than classical computers in certain scenarios.

Python has emerged as a prominent language in the quantum computing landscape, largely due to its extensive library ecosystem and ease of use. Several quantum computing frameworks, such as IBM's Qiskit, Google's Cirq, and Microsoft's Q (with Python bindings), offer robust tools for developing and simulating quantum algorithms. Qiskit, for example, provides a comprehensive suite of tools for constructing quantum circuits, running quantum algorithms on simulators, and accessing real quantum hardware through IBM's cloud-based quantum computing services. This accessibility enables researchers and developers to experiment with quantum algorithms and gain insights into the potential applications of quantum computing in fields like cryptography, optimization, and drug discovery.

However, the advancement of quantum computing also raises important considerations regarding AI ethics and responsible technology use. As the power of computational systems increases, so do the ethical implications of their deployment. AI ethics encompasses a wide range of issues, including data privacy, algorithmic bias, transparency, and accountability. Python, being a central language in the development of AI applications, is deeply intertwined with these ethical considerations. Ensuring that AI systems are designed and used responsibly involves implementing practices that promote fairness, transparency, and privacy.

For instance, addressing algorithmic bias involves analyzing and mitigating biases present in training data and ensuring that models make fair and equitable predictions. Libraries such as Fairness Indicators and AI Fairness 360, both of which integrate with Python, provide tools and frameworks to evaluate and address fairness concerns in machine learning models. Similarly, Python-based tools like Shap and LIME offer methods for interpreting model predictions, thereby enhancing the transparency and interpretability of AI systems. As AI technologies continue to advance, it is crucial to integrate ethical considerations into the development and deployment processes to ensure that these technologies benefit society as a whole.

Looking forward, the future of Python in the tech industry is poised for continued growth and innovation. Python's versatility, readability, and extensive library support have solidified its position as a leading language in various domains, from web development and data science to machine learning and automation. The language's evolving ecosystem, driven by a vibrant community of developers and researchers, contributes to its adaptability and relevance in an ever-changing technological landscape.

One area of growth is the increasing integration of Python with cloud computing platforms. As organizations increasingly adopt cloud services for their infrastructure needs, Python's compatibility with major cloud providers like AWS, Azure, and Google Cloud Platform facilitates the development and deployment of scalable applications. Cloud-native services such as serverless computing and managed machine learning platforms offer opportunities to leverage Python's capabilities in building and deploying applications that can handle large-scale data processing and complex computations.

Furthermore, the rise of containerization and microservices architecture, exemplified by technologies like Docker and Kubernetes, has transformed how applications are developed, deployed, and managed. Python's compatibility with these technologies enables developers to create containerized applications that can be easily scaled, updated, and maintained. The use of Docker for containerization, coupled with Kubernetes for orchestration, provides a powerful combination for managing the lifecycle of Python-based applications in a cloud environment.

In addition to these practical advancements, Python's role in education and research continues to expand. As the language becomes increasingly integrated into academic curricula and research projects, it fosters a new generation of developers and researchers who will drive future innovations. Python's simplicity and effectiveness in teaching programming concepts make it an ideal choice for educational settings, while its robust libraries and frameworks support advanced research in areas such as computational biology, finance, and social sciences.

In summary, the landscape of Python programming is marked by significant advancements and emerging trends that shape the future of technology. From the revolutionary potential of quantum computing to the ethical considerations in AI, Python's adaptability and extensive ecosystem position it as a pivotal tool in addressing complex challenges and driving innovation. As the tech industry evolves, staying abreast of these developments and contributing to the ongoing discourse will be essential for leveraging Python's capabilities and ensuring its continued relevance in the ever-changing technological landscape.

www.ingramcontent.com/pod-product-compliance
Lightning Source LLC
Chambersburg PA
CBHW052145220526
45471CB00004B/1538